The Improvising Society

The Improvising Society

Social Order in a Boundless World

Hans Boutellier

eleven
international publishing

Published, sold and distributed by Eleven International Publishing
P.O. Box 85576
2508 CG The Hague
The Netherlands
Tel.: +31 70 33 070 33
Fax: +31 70 33 070 30
e-mail: sales@budh.nl
www.elevenpub.com

Sold and distributed in USA and Canada
International Specialized Book Services
920 NE 58th Avenue, Suite 300
Portland, OR 97213-3786, USA
Tel: 1-800-944-6190 (toll-free)
Fax: +1-503-280-8832
orders@isbs.com
www.isbs.com

Eleven International Publishing is an imprint of Boom uitgevers Den Haag.

Translated by Kay Richardson, with the assistance of Ian Priestnall

Cover image by Shutterstock, Filipe B. Varela

ISBN 978-94-6236-078-5
ISBN 978-94-6094-825-1 (E-book)

Printed in The Netherlands

For Els, Bas, and Nikki

FOREWORD TO THE ENGLISH EDITION

This book has taken me many places and among interesting groups of people, both in my own land, the Netherlands, and internationally. The lectures, master classes, and workshops in which I have discussed it have taught me a great deal; I gradually began to realize its importance. Many people have an immediate grasp of the idea of the improvising society. They often experience our era as haphazard, disordered, and heavily dependent on their own energy, yet they also see its inherent possibilities. This book has helped them to better understand our world, as they say, and some now even regard it as optimistic.

In today's world we have difficulty formulating grand, comforting ideas. We hear a cacophony of voices and opinions, we see rage and frustration, and observe a lot of ad hoc policy and tentative management. There is a lot of fumbling around without a guiding concept. We can call this improvising, but is there perhaps more order in what we are doing than we think? Perhaps we have missed something. For years I have sought a suitable title to describe this.

The importance of improvisation as a concept dawned on me in 2008 while reading an interview with a jazz guitarist. He referred to his music as "organized freedom." That also describes improvisation, a combination of structure and innovation. A successful improvisation is possibly the highest form of human organization. Improvisation was a way for me to describe today's society as rapidly shifting, complex, in perpetual flux. It shows lesser and greater degrees of success in both consistency and coherence. And it is based on a continuous process of fine-tuning among all identities within an organized context.

Although my express purpose is to present an objective diagnosis, I also confess to harboring a certain hope within that diagnosis. I have tried to present a reasonable description of our current society, without downplaying its problems. New social forms mean new terminology. This book is intended to give a perspective on the opportunities of our time. Society's complexity also contains – as I show – the possibility of finding better and more robust practices. To that end, I devote much attention to public morality, because I regard it a deciding factor in human ordering.

This book has two intellectual sources of inspiration. First is the Verwey-Jonker Institute in the Netherlands, which conducts independent contract research on social issues. I have been the institute's director since 2003. The second source is my academic chair "Security and Citizenship" and its research group at the VU University Amsterdam. This book aims at giving a broader perspective of the whole of projects in which I am involved. Many people have inspired me in this endeavor – too many to list here. I thank my family, who regularly ask me what all my pondering is about. Because occasionally I don't know the answer to that myself, I dedicate this English edition to them, too.

Hans Boutellier
Haarlem, June 2013

TABLE OF CONTENTS

PART I COMPLEXITY WITHOUT DIRECTION

Conditions in our society have changed decisively during recent decades. One now speaks of a network society, which is the result of major processes such as globalization, the rise of individualism, and the dawn of the information age. It is almost impossible to comprehend the consequences of these developments. Enormous uncertainty goes hand-in-hand with embracing these new times. My first basic observation is that many regard these as chaotic times, which leads to two central problems.

First there is a lack of moral clarity. We yearn for direction – in our politics, our institutions, and our personal relationships. Second, it is impossible to comprehend the structure of our society, by which I mean the complexity of its organization, given the current tangle of institutions. Complexity without direction is the hallmark of our society, and it creates a pervasive uneasiness that manifests in antisocial behavior, criminality, excessive stress, fear of the digital world, dissatisfaction, and frustration.

Part One deals with social ambivalences in a world without boundaries. It examines the administrative impotence and societal rage of our era. I also introduce and discuss my central question: How can we imagine social order in a boundless world? Assuming that society is to continue, then some form of organization is needed.

CHAPTER 1

A FIRST EXPLORATION

Several years ago I attended a lecture by an expert in governance who had researched the systems and processes in a large city. He discussed the city's multi-level governance structure, the collaboration between public and private agencies, and the hopeless tangle of projects and initiatives. There was no end to his descriptions of what was going on. We waited for the conclusion, which finally appeared on the last slide of his PowerPoint presentation. His diagnosis was splashed across the screen in capital letters: *complexity*! The expert looked triumphantly around the hall after unveiling his ultimate finding, while the audience stared back at him somewhat dumbfounded. The simple truth is not always intrinsically convincing.

In recent years I have been very involved with representatives from public administration. That was not always an unmitigated joy, but not because these people are unfit or incompetent. The opposite is closer to the truth. There is an abundance of well-educated and good-willed people in public administration, yet they seem to have succumbed to a lack of direction. In our discussions there was often an undertone of "we just don't know any more." Cynicism is not appropriate here; rather, a certain compassion – if I may call it that – seems to be in order. Modern society is so complex that administration often seems to just muddle through. There is an enormous amount of improvisation going on.[1]

It is easy to blame the administrators for not providing leadership, for being too unpredictable, or for lacking integrity. Yet managerial impotence does not develop in a vacuum. It has its counterpart in a much wider area of social uncertainty. Many organizations have difficulty in defining their function, while their professional staff are looking for normative guidance in their work. There are great aspirations and good intentions, but they are matched by insecurity. Professionals feel goaded by their managers to perform, yet often suffer from feelings of performance anxiety.[2] This book discusses the cause of social impotence among managers and professionals: *complexity!*

In such a situation it is tempting to proclaim that it is no longer possible to get things done. That is a popular intellectual position, after the dearth of pretensions from several decades ago. Many intellectuals have left the public arena and become technocrats, or columnists, or fulltime cynics. Administrators, who are in need of a reasonably coherent narrative, have been abandoned and must make do with memories of ideological movements from the previous century, while dealing with demanding citizens and consultants, lots of consultants. It is *not* my intention here to join that last group. Instead, I aspire to discover if there is more order in the current community than we seem to think. The question to ask is how a world without boundaries organizes itself socially.

Of a different order

This book is not just about social order, but about social ordering. The process itself is important. The relatively coherent ideological order of a great deal of the twentieth century has been replaced with other forms. How are we to understand these new forms, which are characterized by great complexity and moral pluralism? It is tempting to speak of chaos, as Boomkens literally does in his book *De nieuwe wanorde* [The new chaos] (2006). I find this approach one-dimensional (and indifferent) because it says nothing about specific attempts to conquer chaos. I assume that social ordering is necessary because it manages to manifest itself – in more or less desirable forms. This means it may be possible to guide it, which in turn implies that it is potentially amenable to government policy.

Social order is a broad concept, with long traditions in philosophy, sociology, and law.[3] I approach the question of social ordering from two perspectives: *moral coherence* and the *institutional design* of society. To my mind, these are the most urgent themes of our time. The moral perspective points to the meaning that others have for us, based on our notion of self, on intuitions about the good life (the classic philosophical question), and what we experience as evil. The Polish sociologist Piotr Stzompka (2002, p. 63) uses the term "moral space," in which social order is realized.

Acknowledging the importance of a moral space goes back to Emile Durkheim (1893), who spoke of the "moral density" of a people as an independent social quality (along with tangible forms such as contact, speech, and action). That this moral space varies across time and culture needs little elucidation. The transition from a rural to an industrialized society has been extensively documented and interpreted.[4] These analyses are always paired with some concern for the moral quality of the new era.

Sztompka (2002, p. 65) lists three recurring concerns. The first is the idea that loss of social ties undermines the quality of society. This is found in sociological literature from Tönnies to Putnam. The second problem is that of a dominant rationality, in which enchantment has disappeared (the iron cage concept). This goes back to Weber and can be found, e.g., in the work of Zygmunt Bauman (see Chapter 2). Third is the idea that a lack of normative structure brings with it meaninglessness and loss of boundaries (anomie). We find this in Durkheim and communitarians such as Etzioni (see Chapter 3).

The development of modernity always imparts a degree of unease to the design of moral space. On the one hand this leads to relativization of the moral theme: It has always been so. On the other hand this historical unease points out its obvious importance: A credible moral structure offers peace and security. It serves as a precondition for social interaction, political activity, and collective action. Moral space needs to be organized if it is to be social. And this is exactly why we seem to have difficulty with a world without boundaries. What can we say about the moral space of our time?

This brings me to the second, or institutional, perspective. Social institutions can be understood as structures and mechanisms that guide the behavior of groups of individuals. They have a goal and permanence, and they rise above individual desires and needs. Countless institutions contribute to the design of moral space: the family, the educational system, administration, religious organizations, and the legal system. Together they form the foundations of society, but I have noted that in reality the load-bearing cohesion of these institutions is coming under stress. Coherence, cooperation, chains and links, and networks – these are the key words in the formula for institutional complexity. And so I examine social ordering, interpreting it as the design of moral space according to organization, content, and process.[5]

Many in sociology have searched for a unifying principle that underlies social order. According to Emile Durkheim, we can choose between God and the community. If God is no longer the legitimizing force for social order, then the community serves as the necessary alternative. Durkheim wrote that in 1906. But if we also lose our faith in community, what alternatives are still available?[6] Is there another option possible – perhaps we've overlooked something! We can cleave to what there once was (God or community) – that's the conservative solution. We can also reconcile ourselves to cosmopolitan chaos, which is the libertarian solution. Or we can try to find another principle of ordering.

Social patterns

A century after Durkheim, our choices are order as previously conceived, chaos, or something else. In this book I explore that third option. With this goal in mind I set forth my intellectual program. It began with my study on public morality in "postmodern times." In *Solidariteit en slachtofferschap* [Solidarity and victimhood] (1993),[7] I came to the conclusion that the core of "postmodern" morality is to be found in rejection. We find one another – under atomizing conditions – in the acknowledgment and recognition of suffering, discrimination, cruelty, or (in a manner of speaking) victimhood. When a higher purpose is missing (or has been privatized), all that is left as a guideline for moral judgments is the capacity for empathy with other people's misery. "Are you suffering?" is the core question of postmodern morality, according to philosopher Richard Rorty (1989). I explore this proposition in relation to the question of criminality.

Since the 1970s, the victim of crime has grown into a moral archetype:[8] an authorized agent of public affairs, whose suffering comprises the stakes for moral superiority, and hence has become a political "figure."[9] This "victimalization" of morality has created a mental breeding ground for the growth of insecurity as a source of discontent and craving. Everyone has the potential to be a victim, or, more importantly, a potential criminal. Criminality is increasingly regarded as a risk, and for that reason is redefined as a security problem. This insight led to the second step in my program. Under the conditions of a risk society (Beck, 1986), "security" gives direction to social discontent and desire.

This situation has two distinct sides. Against a historic and culturally unique freedom to form our own lives – which I call "vitality" – stands the desire for protection, risk management, and security. Our dealings thus fall under the aegis of a *utopian longing*, in which maximum freedom and maximum security must coincide – the safety utopia (Boutellier, 2002).[10] This has consequences for the objectives of the criminal law system, but the effects go much further. "Security" functions like a semantic dragnet, collecting all sorts of reasons for discomfort – from depravity to organized crime, from terrorism to dog poop on public sidewalks.

This striving for security takes on the character of a societal project (Boutellier, 2005). Facilitated by technological developments, security has grown into a vehicle that helps shape society. More specifically, we can see how security relates to the network society, in which solid structures are being replaced with looser bonds. Security seeks to control the fluid structure of society. The next step in the development of this thesis (Boutellier, 2007b) is as follows: A much greater desire is hidden behind the preoccupation with security – a longing for social order. This is an understandable and legitimate need in both a social and a psychological sense.

A community of persons cannot do without social ordering in terms of organization and normative direction. In the past decades the existing order has been seriously shaken up. Not many social structures are left standing. But that is not to say that there have been no replacements. Social reality is renewing itself. My attempt to describe this is built on the culture of victimalization described earlier and the risk society that longs for security. These conditions remain just as relevant as in the past, but the underlying question of social order needs to be understood using different vocabularies.

In a boundless world, social order develops through a multitude of practices, relations, and mentalities, and is characterized by the speed and vitality of the processes. It is paired with strong emotions and social strife – both constructive and destructive. Social order is giving permanent form to relationships among people in "liquid" conditions (Zygmunt Bauman's term; see Chapter 2). Yet a liquid society is not simply liquid. There are relatively solid institutions such as law, business, education, the medical industry, and the physical infrastructure. Schuyt (2006) speaks of "buttresses of the society." These institutions are not inviolable, and even they stand under pressure from the maelstrom of individualization, technological change, and globalization. Yet they are still standing, sometimes because they have braced themselves, and sometimes because they move with the storm.

The new ordering of society, in other words, develops around solid yet adaptive institutions. This means that it is not one-dimensional. The popular image of a horizontal world needs to be expanded by those moments of ordering that call on power, authority, or institutional *gravitas*. A traffic ticket for running a red light is not a horizontal event. The image of a liquid society should be amended by noting that the solidity of institutions has not disappeared, but this solidity has found new patterns in which to function.[11] This is all about the ordering of nodes in a broader environment. Nodes (identities of different weights) point to other nodes (persons, organizations, institutions), and together they form a three-dimensional fabric with centers of gravity that pull and give direction: a network society. But this oft-used concept does not cover the various social tensions involved and how they are structured within it.

Cultural ambivalence

The fabric created by the network society is not solid. There are enwoven flaws, odd patterns, even holes. It is after all created by humans. Networks are social relationships in which power and authority –and the strife surrounding them – play an unabridged role. But their conditions have changed. I use the term "world without boundaries" to refer to globalization, but also to the relatively unstructured space in which this strife takes place. Values, norms, opinions, and emotions move freely without much guidance from ideologies or structures. Coherent world-views are frugal, limited in theme, and often sow confusion. The current process of social ordering is marked by ambivalence. The following is an example.

In 2008 the Netherlands was in thrall to *Fitna*, a film highly critical of Islam made by the anti-immigration Dutch politician Geert Wilders. Indeed, all of Europe held its breath. Embassies were notified of the official Dutch position on the subject, and Dutch expatriates living in Islamic lands were extremely concerned about the consequences, if the film were to be aired. Dutch opinion leaders were quick to tell the world that it was idiotic to be concerned about a film that hadn't even been shown. But perhaps it wasn't so idiotic, given the reactions of fanatical Muslims to the Danish cartoons that had been published earlier. Demonstrations against Western blasphemy did not look terribly appealing.

Wilders was playing with fire in oil-rich lands, and in that sense it was logical to discuss the issue publicly. It was more than just an election stunt, and Wilders got exactly what he wanted. He generated maximum attention for what he considers to be the greatest danger of this era. Islam is the only faith that can sow so much hatred in the West that it creates fear among non-believers.[12] Islamophobia is not totally absurd paranoia; it refers to the real possibility of hate, indiscriminate violence, and well-planned terrorism against Western "decadence." Wilders was even more successful: He had laid bare the fissure in Western relativism.

This cognitive split shows itself in different variations. People defended Wilders' right to make the film, but nobody wanted to broadcast it. Many accused Wilders of being provocative, while at the same time recognizing the risks of a political Islam. Wilders' right to freedom of speech was defended. Liberalism embraces tolerance, but that makes it difficult to combat radicalism. We see the necessity of defending our values, but they hinder us from defending them in absolute terms. Western relativism – a historic high point in civilization – lacks an idiom that can protect itself against being undermined by fundamentalism.

Wilders exposed this essential weakness and called it cowardice. But what Western liberalism must protect is precisely this ability to be "weak" (in this regard see Pels, 2005). The West puts its faith in doubt, pragmatism, and the power of skepticism. This deeply rooted dichotomy cannot bear "truth at any price." It is the foundation of the development of the sciences, democracy, and the emancipation of individuals and societies on the condition that they join the split soul of freedom. We acknowledge the weakness of this position, but are not prepared in principle to transcend it. In a socially liberal context, there is no collective final word, not even a holy one.

There is a saying in Dutch that the soup is never eaten as hot as it is served. When *Fitna* was finally televised, its generalizations about Islam were so unbelievable that no one took the film seriously. It resembled an "agitprop"[13] made by a terrorist cell. Muslims paid little attention to it, and Muslim organizations actively promoted a calm response to it. The incident is characteristic of our time, especially in its symbolism. We wrestle with the question of integration of minorities, but even more with the question of who we really can be in a world without boundaries. This applies to the native Dutch as well as new immigrants, and for all citizens who can be both here and there digitally, and move physically with minimal differences in time, energy, and methods. Human networks demand cohesion among identities.

A question of identity

Many years ago Anthony Giddens (1991) described the current era as late modern, or modernity in a post-traditional phase. The future of children is no longer decided by family history; modern citizens must develop their own identities. Information increases, individual choices increase, and the independence of experts also increases (and with proportional distrust).[14] It is an era of extreme reflexivity, and therein lies the difference with the recently ended emancipatory era. "While emancipatory politics is a politics of life chances, life politics is a politics of lifestyle. . . . It is a politics of self-actualisation in a reflexively ordered environment, where that reflexivity links self and body to systems of global scope" (Giddens, 1991, p. 214).

When Giddens wrote that, the internet was just a toddler. In a digitally unbounded world, identity is even more a core assignment of states, communities, institutions, and individuals. It is difficult to overestimate the "power of identity" (Castells, 2000b; see Chapter 6 of this book). A striking example of this occurred in the Netherlands in 2008, when Máxima, the very popular Argentine-born wife of the Dutch king, said that she had searched for the Dutch identity but had not found it. That was during the presentation of a report subtitled "Identification with the Netherlands" published by a government think tank, the Dutch Scientific Council for Government Policy (2007). According to this report, we identify ourselves through many positions and roles, thus making the idea of a one-sided national identity relative. The think tank advised the government not to harp on the question of national identity too much.

This somewhat obvious statement brought strong reactions aimed at both Máxima and the think tank. Paul Scheffers, an important Dutch publicist, even called it an insult to the Dutch on national television. When the nation-state is under siege on various fronts – from economic globalization, the information society, the European Union, and one million new Dutch citizens – the hope for a national identity (even if no one can define it) grows. In 2006 plans were announced with great fanfare for a national historical museum; those plans (at least for the present) have gone nowhere.

Culture, integration, identity – the great social themes throughout history – are even greater now that they have assumed an unbounded form. After the post-war era of the Dutch welfare state (1950-1990), one had hoped that "the market" would organize social order. Given the current economic crisis, that neoliberal hope is now under enormous pressure. The commercialization during the 1990s had a disjointing rather than ordering effect on social relations. A world without boundaries seems uninhabitable if only its economic meaning is acknowledged – even though the cosmopolitan elite have no problem with this (Cuperus, 2009). The examples given above of cultural disputes typify the unbounded and ambivalent world at the beginning of the twenty-first century. Authors such as Bauman and Giddens do not neglect to emphasize that ours is a time of insecurity. And that has certain consequences.

It has been shown many times by The Netherlands Institute for Social Research that people are satisfied with their own lives, but are concerned about the moral caliber of society in general.[15] This is an expression of longing for normative guidelines, but especially guidelines for others. Apparently most of us create satisfactory environments for ourselves, but have difficulty in placing them within the larger whole. Responsibility for our own actions has been placed squarely on our own shoulders, according to Bauman (1993, p. 31).[16] We have the not insubstantial psychological task of identifying with a variety of roles, positions, and bonds.[17] When self-evident forms of identity are missing, we need to seek shelter (without an address). In that connection, we can speak of psychological *briocolages* or makeshift constructions. We tinker our own coherence together (Turkle, 1984). Most individuals seem to manage this, but they have difficulty imagining the society in which they belong.

The ambivalences of our time put heavy demands on communities, states, neighborhoods, institutions, organizations, families, and individuals. The solutions found for identity insecurity often vary widely. On the one hand we see the hedonistic enjoyment of the body in sports, fashion, and cosmetic surgery. On the other hand we see the body hidden under scarves, voluminous clothing, and even *burqas*. These are examples of the kaleidoscopic images that must be transcended in order to come to a communal representation. There is enormous tension between the fragmenting forces of the outside world and the longing for coherence. We can organize our own environment reasonably well, but we cannot begin to grasp how it fits into the rest of the unbounded world.

Pragmatism pure and simple

Our era has no wide-open perspectives, no grand designs, no epic narratives. The governance of our society is characterized mainly by pragmatism. If nobody knows the answer, then we choose what seems to be "best": good practices, effective interventions, evidence-based policy. We formulate a politics of risk management and crisis management, of managerial problems and relations management, of market forces and freedom of choice. Our politics is procedural, liberal, and mediagenic, or at least it aspires to be so – there are not many decidedly substantive ideals. We let ourselves be led by effectiveness and efficiency,[18] preferably demonstrated by performance indicators, guided by supervision and control, and accompanied by a politics of spin doctors and sound bites.

This "pragmacracy" stands in sharp contrast to the quest for norms, values, and meaning that is also currently underway. The number of options available to us is historically unprecedented. Our discontent (which has been so often observed and researched) might stem from the fact that we cannot be anything other than pragmatic. That is characteristic of the ambivalence in the Western world: the realization that we have not succeeded in defining our social relations, despite all our other successes. We observe a perpetual shortage or even a human surplus

(Vuyk, 2002), yet there is no reassuring thought about who we are or could possibly be. What terms can we use to think about the social ordering that shapes our life projects?

In this book I attempt to describe the empirical ordering of our current society, or (perhaps better put) the process in which it is realized. In doing so, I become part of the pragmatism, but I do take up a special position. Instead of asking the practical question "what works?"[19] I ask the empirical-analytical question, "what is at work here?" In that sense one can speak of metapragmatism. I examine the manner in which social ordering occurs. Understanding that process better is an alternative to the politics of angst and the alarming reactions to it (Duyvendak et al., 2008). Attempts to create order are legitimate and necessary, and sometimes take on distorted forms. How can we interpret this in a reassuring manner?

Among other things, I hope to show that ordering takes new forms, which at the same time have grown from the historical actuality of institutions. Ordering can be contingent as well as structured. Sometimes there is a conscious intent to create order, but more often we are not really aware of what is happening. This makes it difficult to distinguish between what is desirable or unavoidable, and vice versa. Changes occur in such a turbulent context that sometimes they are barely noticeable and do not set us thinking. Anyone who discovers a pattern of ordering in a complex society, deciphers how it comes into being, and can then change it, is quite the wonder worker.

We are witnessing continual attempts to create order within an apparently chaotic context. Some attempts take the form of an ordering offensive, for example in the area of security (see Chapter 4). That can be regarded as "new social engineering" (see, for example, Van Asselt, 2009, or Frissen, 2007) or as a form of "social hypochondria" that results in exclusion (e.g., Schinkel, 2008). In my opinion, these judgments are too general to be relevant. At least, some sort of social ordering is too important for society, and the actual ordering process is so multifaceted and complex that totalitarian control is not an immediate concern.

It may be better to try to understand the ordering processes in the hope of being able to manage them somewhat.[20]

Social continuity

To avoid any misunderstanding: This book is not meant to provide a single comforting thought, but instead offers perhaps a few useful phrases when thinking about social order. And within this conceptual *framing* a theoretical problem[21] is embedded. My vocabulary is both descriptive and normative. To state my intentions even more strongly: I provide commentary, but also a glimmer of hope. By articulating the actual process of social ordering, I also create a perspective that, in my opinion, fits the current context. I search for a viable position between David Hume's famous *is* and *ought* dichotomy that might be described as *could be*. This is how I hope to contribute to what I call *social continuity*. That concept refers to a robust social connection that is both stable and flexible, thus guaranteeing its survival into the future.

This criterion of social continuity establishes a relationship with sustainability in the ecological movement. And the concept of continuity also contains a subtle reference to economic order, in which continuity – more so than profit maximization – can be regarded as a goal. Yet after invoking these two major policy fields – the economy and the environment – I also depart from them. These are areas of related interest, but I am not going to explore them further. This book is concerned with social order and how it defines moral space from the perspective of the continuity of society. Society is understood as the totality of relationships between people that are both formally and informally arranged, and are also self-evident.

Social continuity forms a motif around which order can be realized, but it is not a guiding concept. In its application it can work defensively, or be too intrusive. It can be liberal as well as conservative. It shows the importance of the relationship between ordering and chaotic forces. It is about the conflict between barbarity and civilization, between pleasure and reality, between spontaneity and security. This dichotomy continues to play itself out in new conditions. In a world without boundaries – geographical and mental – it takes on the form of a permanent improvisation process. That is the central thesis of this book. And these improvisations vary from fanatic structuring to desperately silly tinkering, from brilliant harmony to just messing around.

The concept of an improvising society gives a framework in which the moral incoherence and the institutional complexity of our time can be better understood. In a normative sense, I regard improvisation as the promise of *organized freedom*.[22] This dynamic rises above the image of chaos versus order. In the concept of "freedom" – both positive and negative – we recognize the grand premise of the rule of law, in which every citizen is equal and can live his or her life spontaneously and without arbitrary government intervention. And the word "organized" reminds us of the imperfection of that same individual, who must live in dependence on fellow individuals and the ordering necessary to make that possible – in the community, society, and the network society.

New conditions require new forms of ordering. After the community (*Gemeinschaft*), with its mechanical order, and society (*Gesellschaft*), with its organic order, we could speak of a *Netzschaft*, or "net-ity," which realizes its social order via improvisation. A new form of society is developing within network structures – a social ordering by nodes and the relations between them. These can take on any imaginable shape, depending on the movements of the adjoining (horizontal and vertical) connections. I have much to say about the characteristics of this nodal universe, but at present let me just note the following. Networks can be seen *not* as the cause but as the solution to complexity, provided they are given normative direction from explicit identities.

This introductory chapter has touched briefly on several of the themes to be discussed in the following chapters. The first part follows with a further diagnosis of the world without boundaries. In Chapter 2 I describe its "psychology." Many experience it as chaotic, and some are overwhelmed by it. I deal with problems such as criminality, annoyance and cyber-hatred, and their interpretation. In so doing, I look at the frayed edges of society, where social order is almost nonexistent. This is where the excesses that seem to dominate the images of the current society seem to occur. I try to understand this in terms of a failure of civilization in its disciplinary and especially its identity-affirming significance.

The second part describes the ordering programs that have been used to rein in complexity without direction. In Chapters 3, 4, and 5, I describe a program of civilization in terms of values and norms, a security program for risk management, and a program for active citizenship. Together their mutual aspects form a picture of the social ordering offensive in the first decade of the twenty-first century. This offensive has both substantial and hazardous aspects, in the form of overestimation and missed opportunities, with both pleasant results and hilarious characteristics. Even these programs cannot avoid the improvisational character of the network society.

Part Three sketches the contours of the improvising society. Chapter 6 considers the conditions that led to a complex world without direction, based on Manuel Castells' work on the information era, among others. In the same chapter, I show how, even in apparent chaos, order can emerge, or (more accurately) can be observed. I look for ideas and concepts from complexity theories in science. Chapter 7 deals more specifically with the problem of ordering in human systems. I consider the functions of control and trust, which are anchored in the law, social regulations, and "the domain of the self-evident."

In Chapter 8 I discuss the concept of improvisation and its essential characteristics. Improvisation is simultaneously organization, content, and process. It makes both the fluid character of current society and the more robust forms of organization understandable. The essence can be found in the fine-tuning. Direction and organization are in the core functions of institutions. I conclude with an epilogue, in which I give my scientific justifications.

CHAPTER 2

BETWEEN RAGE AND IDENTITY

When Ulrich Beck launched the concept of a risk society in 1986, he obviously had no idea what form it would take. The old society had worked on the principle of sharing what was scarce. Yet the ideologically driven politics to which that principle belonged, according to Beck, shifted to a completely different dynamic. New technologies were leading to problems that could no longer be understood in terms of "distribution." Beck's statements that "smog is democratic" and "radioactivity is invisible" neatly summarized what society was facing. Invisible risks that were difficult to comprehend became important in governance.[1] Risk management, rather than steering society in a desired direction, has become the main theme in politics.

Much has changed since Beck's book first appeared. The concept of the risk society seemed to fit other relatively ungovernable problems – globalization with its accompanying migrations, and individualization, which eroded social bonds. Living in society became more of a free enterprise inspired by a somewhat myopic market mentality, with a policy based on risk analysis and asset management. People developed suitable lifestyles to fit these conditions. The social boundaries of the past lost their relevance. The risk society became a "risk culture" that bounced back and forth between the desire for a full life and the fear that things were out of control.

In the twenty-first century the risk society became even more tangible. The airplanes crashing into the World Trade Center in 2001 brought an end to thinking in terms of invisible risks. In the Netherlands, the rise in popularity and the very public murder of Pim Fortuyn, a flamboyant populist politician, made the risk society so palpable that it lost all meaning as a concept. Then the murder in broad daylight of Theo van Gogh, a bitingly sarcastic, high-profile social critic, really sounded the death knell. The risks in society – even in Holland – had become very real indeed. Van Gogh's murder on November 2, 2004 and the commotion surrounding it were riddled with ambivalence (see also Buruma, 2006). When Job Cohen, the mayor of Amsterdam, tried to address a crowd at a memorial gathering (despite having himself frequently been a target of Van Gogh's barbs), he was jeered. Van Gogh had been both adored and hated – often at the same time. For many, reading Van Gogh's provocative and frequently outrageous columns had been a guilty pleasure.

An unheard-of resentment began to grow in Dutch society under the catch-all phrase "great discontent" – people were against "strangers," against "politics," against institutions, and against each other. Holland lost its innocence during the first decade of the twenty-first century. Even stronger, it seemed as though Holland had once again taken the lead in sharpening social and/or multicultural differences.[2] In this chapter I examine the psychological aspects of the world without boundaries. Where there is complexity without direction, rage and frustration are lurking. That is why I choose as my starting point the concept of the "liquid society" as developed by the Polish-British sociologist Zygmunt Bauman.[3] I discuss the cultural consequences of this, and then the resultant relation between present-day rage and the condition of our civilization.

Liquid modern

Contemporary culture, according to Bauman, is so unregulated that a great deal of angst and insecurity has been brought into play. "The discontents of postmodernity arise from a kind of freedom of pleasure-seeking which tolerates too little individual security" (Bauman, 1997, p. 3). In other words, it is a treacherous kind of freedom that is now common, a freedom that generates fear.[4] It is the freedom of consumerism, which ultimately leads us to cash in our individual freedom for individual security. Bauman explores this theme further in his "liquid" books. He calls a society "liquid modern" if the conditions in which its members act change so quickly that behavior cannot be consolidated into habits or routines (Bauman, 2005, p. 1).

In Bauman's alarmist musings, we are doomed to a life without peace and normal routines, because what is new today is no longer valid tomorrow. With the concept of "liquid" Bauman succeeds in putting into words that radical difference from previous forms of modernity. He contrasts it with the concept of "solid."[5] To characterize this new phase, he points to concepts such as individualization, globalization, and technological change. We need not expect a careful analysis of their overlap from him. Instead he concentrates on the consequences for Western culture and the manner in which its members give form to their lives.

High intensity, rapidly changing conditions, and superficial relationships lead to permanent insecurity. The only security is the need to continually begin anew. Not preservation and continuity, but rather forgetting, deleting, abandoning, and moving on are what make the liquid life (Bauman, 2003, p. 2).[6] In a liquid society there are no criteria for how we should behave and what quality means. There is no striving for a normal condition, and no end station. Bauman uses the example of "fitness." Not only do we want to be healthy, we also want to be fit, yet fitness is a subjective experience that has no objective criteria (2000, p. 77). The same reasoning applies to longing for security. Being both fit and safe are the wishful dreams of fluid identities; because neither has an end destination, they form a source of constant longing.

Bauman regards "shopping" as the archetype of life in a liquid society. Freedom in such a society means, among other things, "freedom to shop" (2000, p. 88). The drive behind this fanatical buying behavior is not necessity but longing, understood as wishful fantasy (2000, p. 73). Shopping malls are an almost perfect realization of the longing for both freedom and security (see also Van Steden, 2009). Protected by private security officers, we delude ourselves that we are absolutely free, on the condition that we can spend money. The freedom of selection is overwhelming, but the time involved is short. What is in today will be old-fashioned tomorrow (with the possibility that it will be hip again the day after tomorrow, just slightly different).

We want to get as many lives as we can out of one body (like in a computer game). In such an environment, loyalty is more a cause for shame than for pride ("a teacher for twenty years – really?!?") This is not a culture of learning and accrued knowledge, but rather one of discontinuity, forgetting, and beginning again (Bauman, 2003, p. 62). Progress summons up mainly fear – of loss, of being left behind, of becoming superfluous. It is that nauseous feeling of missing the train. The fear of becoming "redundant" can only be held at bay by continuously producing. "Liquid life means constant self-scrutiny, self-critique and self-censure. Liquid life feeds on the self's dissatisfaction with itself" (2003, pp. 10-11). This permanent dissatisfaction works like a *perpetuum mobile*. The battle to be unique is the motor behind mass production and mass consumption (2003, pp. 24-25).

Identity and community

In order to understand the psychosocial effects of the liquid Western society, Bauman regularly refers to the solid structures of the past (2007, p. 7, e.g.). Earlier modernity (post-Enlightenment) was defined by patterns, codes, and rules, to which one could conform or not, but they provided stable points of orientation. Such orientation points barely exist now. The weaving of social patterns has become a matter of individual responsibility. Social context is less structured, less hierarchical, and less self-evident.

That also describes the conditions of individualization. "To put it in a nutshell, 'individualisation' consists of transforming human 'identity' from a 'given' into a 'task' and charging the actors with the responsibility for performing the task and for the consequences . . . of their performance" (2000, p. 31f.). According to Bauman, we are witnessing "an unprecedented freedom of experimenting . . . and coping with [its] consequences." Not because we like this, but because we cannot do anything else in liquid conditions. "Individualisation is here to stay" (2000, p. 37). Radical individualization results in a different experience of public space, which forms a giant screen on which the individual can project his or her personal experience (2000, p. 39).

And so the chasm grows between the individual *de jure* (the citizen) and the individual *de facto* (the living being). Empirical individuality seems to have outgrown the jacket of legal citizenship.[7] A liquid society gives plenty of room for expression and longings that are beyond the traditional norms of conformity. That has consequences for "the society," which is in fact based on conformity. Liquid society leads to detachment, deviation, escapism, and the pursuit of individual identity (2000, p. 120). Collectivity and community are not self-evident, but must be created. And because there are no communal goals, this takes place among shared enemies. They are a form of self-protection.[8]

Such "explosive communities" often have a forced, temporary, or fleeting character. Bauman uses terms such as "carnival communities" and "cloakroom communities" interchangeably. They imitate "real" communities that are all-encompassing and sustainable, yet they offer little security. That is why Bauman speaks of the central emotional state in a liquid society as being *Unsicherheit*, a concept he regards as an amalgamation of the English words *insecurity*, *uncertainty*, and *unsafety*.[9] When *Unsicherheit* is dominant in a community, then life does not feel "law-bound and law-abiding, [a] logical, consistent and cumulative chain of actions," but more like a game in which everyone holds his or her cards close to the vest (2000, p. 137).

The current communitarian longing is seen as a rational (but illusory) reaction to the crisis in the public space (2000, p. 108). It explains the rise in nationalism, conservatism, and gated communities.[10] The liquid community prefers the individual above the citizen, and when a sense of community is sought, it often takes on flawed forms – temporary, fundamentalist, explosive, sequestered. These are all manifestations of human bonds in which relations are strained and trust becomes more or less forced. We must learn to walk on quicksand, Bauman warns us in the dramatic conclusion of *Liquid Life*. For Bauman, education is the last whisper of hope in forming fully conscious and self-aware citizens. "We need lifelong education to give us choice" (Bauman, 2005, p. 128), yet it remains unclear how to get such a project off the ground.

A second life

In his merciless descriptions of liquid modernity, Bauman shows how social order and citizenship (community and identity) are being slowly dragged into the maelstrom of globalizing capitalism. It is a culture with a murderous tempo that carries a serious risk that the individual will be tossed out of the system ("trash"). The liquid world Bauman sketches has few moral anchor points left. The solid institutions have melted, and commerce has no moral scruples. It seems justified to speak of a culture that makes people susceptible both to transgressing the norms and/or being afraid of doing so. Criminality, in that sense, is a hallmark of today's culture, and that also applies to the obsessive need for protection from it.

This gives reason to further explore the relation between culture and criminality, an area recently revived under the name *cultural criminology*. In one of the first programmatic approaches to this field, Ferrell and Sanders (1995) noted three correlations between (sub)culture and criminality. First, there is a correlation between certain criminal identities and the associated cultural style (for example, gangster rap). The second is the reverse: cultural expressions are claimed by certain criminal groups. In this case some bands – even without wanting such patronage – are appreciated by neo-Nazis and skinheads (Brown, 2004). In both forms, criminality is a question of lifestyle: "Much of this subcultural meaning, action, identity and status is organized around style – that is, the shared aesthetic of the subculture's members" (Ferrell & Sanders, 1995, p. 5).

Third, Ferrell and Sanders noted the process of cultural criminalization (p. 11) in which criminality or deviant behavior is accorded a certain public meaning. The same is true for the opposite – the fight against crime, e.g., police culture. The media plays a major role in the representation of crime and crime-fighting, and its appreciation by the public (in both dramatic television series and crime documentaries). In this context, criminality seems to be a "coproduction" of behavior and culture. You cannot understand one without the other, and yet criminality in a liquid context is something other than cultural style or coproduction.

Mike Presdee, in *Cultural criminology and the carnival of crime* (2000), examines the issue further. He begins with the observation that current culture is so saturated with violence and transgressions against the norm that it sometimes seems like there is nothing else (p. 3). He ascertains that "excitement, even ecstasy (the abandonment of reason and rationale)" is the goal of criminal "performance" (pp. 7ff.). Presdee emphasizes that criminality and violence can be "enjoyable," and should be understood as "a valuable consumer entertainment commodity" in today's society, and refers to the carnival-like character of much of today's criminality.

Carnival is timeless, and is understood in general as a temporary reversal of the social order. Yet in current culture, carnival is everywhere and nowhere: in satires, novels and films, in body modification, S&M, dance parties, drug abuse, gang rituals, and extreme sports (p. 47). Deviance has become the norm. Borrowing from the work of literary critic Mikhail Bakhtin (1984), Presdee introduces the concept of a "second life": "that part of life that is inaccessible and untouchable to the 'official' world . . . . it is the realm of resentment and irrationality *par excellence* and also the realm of much crime" (2000, p. 8). These carnival-like expressions are "excused" – not permanently and not everywhere, but in the openings that the "normal" first life offers.[11]

The second life has gained a certain status in the entertainment world, the media, night life, and on the internet. Presdee asks us to consider the trademarks of a culture whose doors are wide open for individual emotions, primal lust, and norm violations. "Learning must be fun, poverty must be fun, housework must be fun and as in *Clockwork orange* . . . violence, crime and disorder must be fun" (p. 63). The "consumption of criminality" here seems to be a merciful state of irresponsibility. Presdee regards this desire for extreme forms of popular and personal pleasure as going against the grain of an increasing rationalization (Chapter 9). The second life is no longer a secret condition, but a legitimate part of one's identity that may be regularly displayed in public.

Consumptive narcissism

With Bauman we saw that identity and community have become an individual matter. With a shortage of moral anchor points, according to Presdee, space is created for the formation of a second life of permanent "fun" and norm violations. Within such a context, certain persons can literally get lost in the consumptive liquid world. Hall et al. (2008) gave a sordid image of this.[12] Ethnographic research was done among lower-class youth in the neighborhoods of Carvill in Newcastle and North River and Southfield in Sunderland (both in northeast England). The traditional "working class identity" in these areas has given way to new forms of marginalization that are all about wanting to take part in the consumer market.

The authors paint a picture of amoral violence and drug abuse in an underclass that is involved in a battle to "count for something." Their fear of becoming superfluous ("trash") is the motive for a hedonistic lifestyle: "to have a box-fresh pair of Nikes meant a significant boost to self-esteem" (p. 49). Everything is geared to being "in" through clothing, luxury articles, and hip gadgets. The researchers found no signs of identification with their fellow partners in misfortune, the poor, or other "losers." Their goal in life is to be able occasionally to enter the consumers' paradise. At work here is a kind of consuming fetishism that is rooted in an unattainable, imaginary ideal-ego of participating in the greatest good, consumptive prosperity.[13]

This kind of image of identity does not know how to convert itself into a concrete goal or constructive image of its own existence – into an "I-ideal." The superego seeks pleasure in place of civilization, an argument we came across earlier in Bauman. Feelings of worthlessness are combined with a driving hedonistic consumerism.[14] It is a desire for sublime experiences that can only be fantasized about and are rarely within reach.

Lack of norms goes hand in hand with conformity in regard to the consumptive culture. The second life has become the first lifestyle within this criminal underclass.

Beneath the many quotes and descriptions of this youthful underclass lies a sharp commentary from the authors about the neoliberal trend toward consumer capitalism in the 1990s that was inspired by the American counterculture.[15] The authors agree with Heath and Potter (2004) that the "counterculture became consumer culture." Counterculture representatives have mistakenly lumped social criticism and deviant behavior together,[16] but resistance to domination is different from doing what you feel like (p. 105). The counterculture is the ideal breeding ground for "consumerization of the means of identity" (p. 108). It is difficult to escape the temptations of the consumer society, especially if that is the only way to be somebody.

According to Hall et al. there is an odd tension in the consumer society: one feels the need to be unique through conforming completely. The traditional psychosocial mechanisms of prohibition, repression, and guilt have been so disrupted that the idea of a "community" has dissolved. Everything is allowed; nothing is embarrassing. In such a subculture there are no ideas of social justice, solidarity, and combating social exclusion, but rather a Hobbesian war of everybody against everybody (p. 192). Criminal interviewees present an odd mix of fatalism and optimism, hoping for the one lucky shot that will vault them into the consumers' elite.

The radical analysis of Hall and his colleagues bears certain marks of hyperbole. Yet the quotes and descriptions of the mental state of the young adults they studied are disturbing. They fit the turbulent image of Bauman's liquid community, and they are also in line with my findings regarding "dissatisfied citizens" (De Gruijter et al., 2010). They also allow insight into the far-reaching effects of the globalized consumer economy for social underclasses, and as such are meaningful for society as a whole. While Bauman sketched the cultural contours of the world without boundaries in broad strokes, this analysis offers a look at its outer fringes.

Resentment and recognition

The image that arises from the ideas developed so far is one of alienated individuals who no longer have a sense of belonging to a community, let alone any desire to participate in it. This rather desolate image raises the question of what motivates a lonely person beyond designing a life devoted to maximum pleasure. To explain the frustrated drive to distinguish oneself as unique, Hall and his colleagues mention Plato's idea of *thymos* – personal pride and the will to be recognized – which motivates human behavior alongside reason and desire (pp. 171, 174). They consider this motivating factor as having been contaminated by the culture of consumption that has taken on infantile, narcissistic traits.[17] What does this extreme form of *thymos* teach us about the more general psychology of a world without boundaries?

To examine the will to recognition further, I refer to Peter Sloterdijk's book *Rage and Time* (English edition, 2010). Sloterdijk shows that rage from wounded pride has been a driving psychological force throughout collective history. He calls his work a "psychopolitical investigation." The Greeks praised rage as the motivating force of heroes. They demanded their right to exist and hunted down anyone who denied it. Unlike virtue, rage did not hesitate – "The enraged attack knows where it wants to hit" (p. 10). From a historical perspective, Sloterdijk shows how the affect "rage" has been dismantled by Christianity, while taking on revolutionary forms in Nazism and communism.

Thymotics is a denominator for individuality, pride, courage, resolution, worthiness, honor, indignation, combativeness, revenge, and self-respect. It is beyond the erotic, which deals with loss and longing. Thymotics shows who a person is (and not what he or she lacks) and rage is the result of wounding it. In Christianity rage is the domain of sin, in psychoanalysis that of neurosis, and in the market that of consumption. Proud egoism was rediscovered by Nietzsche as "the best of human possibilities" (p. 16). Although the nation-state of the nineteenth century led to a new appreciation of *thymos*, according to Sloterdijk it became submerged again by the eroticization of the human image.

Sloterdijk thinks it is time to develop anew a psychology of self-esteem (p. 18). A key role in that will be "recognition" as "the most important pivot on which interthymotic relations turn" (p. 33). The civilization of the *thymos* in nation-states was ultimately a grand failure – the twentieth century experienced enormous catastrophes, a rage-economy of planned explosions (p. 25f.). That came to an end after the fall of the Berlin Wall, but this "end of history"[18] meant the beginning of "currents of free-floating dissatisfaction" (p. 39), a point also made by Fukuyama, whose thesis that we are at the "end of history," according to Sloterdijk, has been unjustly ignored. "Especially in a world of universally amended liberties, human beings cannot cease to strive for recognition manifested in prestige, wealth, sexual advantages, and intellectual superiority" (p. 40).

Because these goods are scarce, a reservoir of envy and discontent begins to fill up. "The more 'a society' is satisfied in its basic features, the more colorfully all against all will flourish" (p. 40). Culture, media, and sport offer new possibilities for recognition, but the losers – and certainly those who are "really disadvantaged" – are not silent. They turn not only against the winners, but also against the rules and politics. Sloterdijk emphasizes that hatred and resentment are not new phenomena, although one might once have thought their end was in sight. All cultures need systems to tend the "wounds" of human traumas, humiliations, and frustrations, namely: protest, accountability, settlement, reflection, internalizing, and judicial procedures.[19]

Sometimes resentment builds up to the point that a legitimate outburst occurs – a transformation of acute rage into an act of revenge. "We have entered an era without rage collection points of global perspective. Neither in heaven nor on earth does anyone know what can be done with the 'just anger' of the people (p. 183). What remains are a whisper of discontent and isolated acts of protest. This "dispersion of forces is in stark contrast to the ubiquitous rumor that the world is increasingly interconnected by new media" (p. 184). Sloterdijk does not think highly of the network society's possibilities. The absence of globally accepted ideals leaves us with only "the relentlessly soft center" (p. 185).

"[I]n all of these features is an element of 'anger about what is in fact," a form of "hatred against everything that functions" (Enzensberger, 1992; cited by Sloterdijk, 2010, p. 183). There is talk of "hostility against the world and being as a whole" – an *Internationale* of self-haters" (p. 276f.). And Sloterdijk is not afraid of the clout of political Islam. It is focused in principle on the past and can only lead to outbreaks of violence, fear of which can bring about a sort of pseudo-solidarity, with security as the dominant theme. The "war on terror" cannot be won, and therefore neither does it need to be ended. The danger inherent in this is that post-democratic conditions come to be accepted. What concerns me in all these deliberations is that a world without boundaries has too little resonance for many people to be able to recognize their identities.

The frustrated self

The liquid community of Bauman creates a cultural environment that makes it difficult to be a person who "counts." It is a world in which consumption serves as a source of recognition – with all the frustrations that brings with it. The *thymos* offers, through recognition and self-respect, the potential to "be." In an ideological sense, a social-liberal environment gives the freedom to realize one's own life project. Although the possibilities to do so are not available to everyone, they are for the majority, and the individual is often happy with his or her own life. That raises the question of the more general value of the analyses sketched out above. Shouldn't we look at the differences, sort them into categories, point out the incidental, and relativize? In principle that is true, but the effects of frustrated *thymos* dominate our social representations. We are deathly afraid of other people's rage, and there are always reasons to be so.

Terrorist attacks abroad, two political assassinations in the Netherlands, an assault on the Dutch royal family in 2009, and threats, many enraged threats – these are reason enough to speak of a troubled civilization. My own research has shown that the number of threats against Dutch politicians runs into the hundreds (Verwey-Jonker Instituut, 2010). Many of the threats are against a handful of politicians, but there are also some threats against many. In most instances it consists of "average" hate mail, but sometimes there is real physical danger. A relatively new phenomenon in the Netherlands is that bus drivers are spat at and ambulance crews attacked. These are isolated incidents, but their frequency makes it possible to speak of "structural incidents" (Rosenthal, 1988).

The statistics present a somewhat ambivalent picture. According to population research, criminality is declining, violence is somewhat reduced, yet the number of violent thefts is increasing.[20] But violence, criminality in general, and antisocial behavior are no longer just a matter of statistics and an objective reaction to those statistics. The reactions are now just as fierce as the incidents. One fourth of the victims of nightlife violence have themselves had previous encounters with the police (Bervoets et al., 2008). Citizens are increasingly using the internet to issue their own condemnations (Hammer, 2009), by threatening "criminal" politicians, naming and shaming convicted pedophiles, and accusing specific persons.

Looking for linear explanations in this spiral of activity, outrage, and reaction has a touch of naiveté about it, and analyzing the factual trends smacks of impotence. The situation is far more complex. On the basis of the above thoughts about rage in a community without boundaries, I dare to propose the following. Our obsession with criminality, stress, violence, rage, insecurity, and threats has to do with recognition and self-respect – the lessons of *thymos*. From the perspective of the perpetrators there is a frustrated will to be counted; from the perspective of the law abiders there is recognition that the status quo is good as it is. We need the incentive of insecurity in order to avoid vanishing into a globalized oblivion. If no one tells us who we are – God the Father, the prime minister, the teacher, or any other compelling ideologist – then we must do it for ourselves. We justify our lack of values by either having none or deploring their absence.

The controversial Dutch artist Tinkebell (& Vogelaar, circa 2009) published a book, or artwork, composed of information found on the internet about persons who had sent her hate mail.[21] The contrast between the everyday individuals (often young women) and the mud they were slinging via their keyboards is fascinating. Judging from the photos and the personal information, one cannot speak of a psychological disorder. The hate mail could have come from a neighbor or a colleague, or perhaps even from you, dear reader. The Dutch newspaper *Het Parool* (May 23, 2009) published a letter from a self-confessed writer of hate mail, in which she justifies her right to pen such vicious indictments. At work here is the desire to be "right," and the "rightness" of her own judgment justifies the hatred, the violence, the short fuse, and all the reactions it stirs up.

The veneer of civilization may be thin, historically speaking, but it has vanished completely on the internet. This is possible due to erosion in three areas. First, it is technically possible to remain anonymous while verbally berating someone online: "I'll say what I think because I can." It is also acceptable to insult someone, to point out differences, and to laugh at handicaps or an unusual nose: "I'll say what I think because it's allowed." In Dutch show business, this kind of behavior began with stand-up comedians; now, thanks to the internet, it is part of the culture. And then the erosion goes deeper: "I'll say what I think because I must." Forget about the hypocritical, politically correct cover-ups. Having no "manners" is living for real. Free speech has no limits, because expressing oneself is not only possible, it is allowed and a necessity. The internet is the perfect amoral space in the world without boundaries in which individuals roam freely. Muslim youths in search of answers can find their jihadists, men their daily dose of porno, and the raging masses their hate objects.

It seems as though the human spirit has externalized all its polymorphous perversity (Freud), and the internet is the testing ground for real life, where we can watch the bomb explode with some regularity. Arie Kruglanski et al. (2009), who researched the motives of suicide terrorists, regard the "quest for personal significance" as the deciding factor in suicidal terrorism. The suicide terrorist is willing to offer his existence, his "I," in order to give it meaning. These are isolated incidents, of course, but extremely important ones. A lack of moral boundaries – values, norms, customs, and manners – explains much about our obsession with violence, hate, and excess.

Some kind of civilizing buffer of customs and manners is needed to keep our reactions somewhat under control. This is the conservative analysis (see Chapter 3), yet something far more substantial is going on. The lack of boundaries ultimately creates a lack of recognition. To experience a sense of identity, we need to be addressed. We want to be seen, heard, and even corrected. That is the source of the current rage – feeling superfluous, unnoticed, passed over.

We have arrived at the remotest corners of the world without boundaries, where we find an extreme form of consuming narcissism. I described that earlier as a symptom of a liquid community that has no anchor points. We are not talking about a simple lack of discipline, but rather a lack of a validating function. The core of civilization is every person's claim to identity. It is not evil per se that we see, but the unacknowledged will or need to "be." The layout of moral space rapidly becomes too confining for certain groups, at some points in time, and in various places. And yet there is danger in the compelling analyses of Bauman, Hall and his colleagues, and Sloterdijk. They offer little vision of new forms of ordering and identification, and it is important to search carefully for these, in order to be able to see the stability that is also apparently hidden in the community.

Cultural criticism can quickly take on the character of a paralyzing pessimism in which almost no starting points for constructive activity can be found, yet there is a palpable and real need to act. For example, it is not an appealing thought for parents to bring their children up in constant insecurity. One could even ask if the concept of "liquid" is adequate to describe the current situation in society. It is impossible to maintain that everything that once was "solid" has now dissolved. This applies not only to the manner in which many communities organize themselves, but also to institutions, from education to the law, which are maintaining themselves against the strong current of liquid living. Against this backdrop, in Part Two, I will explore three attempts to counter complexity without direction.

PART II THREE PROGRAMS FOR SOCIAL ORDER

When complexity is the problem, order is the answer. I describe three organizational approaches based on civilization, security, and citizen participation. Of course these "programs" are not unique to our era; they have dominated social policy for decades. Occasionally they resulted in desperate attempts that were doomed from the beginning, but successes were also fairly common. The discussion on civilization is tinged with nostalgia for times past, even reaching back to the classical age. This longing for "the good old days" is based on the hope that a comprehensive moral appeal is still possible, but in the Netherlands this has degenerated into an ultimately futile debate about norms and values. Such has been the trend in conservative thought over the last few decades. The "civilization defensive" represents the desire for great moral themes (values, norms, and virtues) and functions as a mirror held up to society, but its ineffectiveness tends to breed resentment.

One perspective that does give direction can be found in the desire for security, which has its moral origins in criminal law. There is general agreement on this, although the criminal justice system itself is regarded with ambivalence. The function of the law may be cherished, but its organization is distrusted. As a regulating body, the criminal legal system is simply inadequate. Instead, preventive thinking has increasingly come to dominate social policies for safety.

Finally, there is an appeal to citizens for active participation. The authorities regard citizens as both "problem" and "solution," an ambivalent attitude that often forces citizens into an uncomfortable bind. This gives rise to the slippery question of what one should expect from citizens, as well as its corollary, what do citizens want from their government. The central missing element here is a coherent common narrative from the authorities, the experts, and the citizens. What is needed is a moral appeal to citizens to develop it themselves.

CHAPTER 3

THE DUTCH "CULTURAL WAR"

In the first decade of the twenty-first century, suddenly it was all about being "civilized" again – that is to say, about the decline of civilization and attempts to restore it. In the Netherlands, the political resurrection of Jan Peter Balkenende – the seemingly squeaky clean and "fair-haired" leader of the Christian Democratic party – as prime minister in 2002 took place under the banner of "norms and values." Although that theme had been launched earlier by Balkenende's Christian Democratic Appeal party, the CDA,[1] Balkenende was the first prime minister to speak out unabashedly in favor of policy from a moral perspective. Various attempts were made to give solid form to the debate he was trying to start. The Scientific Council for Government Policy, or WRR, released a report (2004); there were European debates (*Nexus* 40, 2004); and there was the oft-repeated slogan "decency is a must" (*fatsoen moet je doen*). Yet none of these efforts led to substantial policy actions, as we shall see.

The norms-and-values project as such seems to have failed – unless we regard Balkenende's fourth cabinet as the apotheosis of the moral agenda. Max Pam, a prominent publicist, referred to that cabinet as a "schoolmarm" or "nanny" cabinet,[2] a description nicely illustrated by the liberal weekly *Revu* (December 2008). "Nothing's allowed nowadays" was the title of a laundry list of prohibitions that the government had recently debated and decided on, e.g., *burqas*, fish bowls (because they are not a healthy environment for goldfish), and smoking. Mature and immature, national and local, barely whispered and assertively proposed, there were in total sixty prohibitions in 2008.

This count may not be exact, but it does nicely indicate the mood in Holland at the end of the first decade of the new century.

A moralizing wind was sweeping across the nation, and of course that also called forth a corresponding countermovement. I regard this attempt at moralizing as part of a broader cultural offensive. Included in the issues were compulsory parenting classes, reducing the number of Dutch "coffee shops" (legal outlets for marijuana), reducing alcohol abuse, prohibiting smoking, using breathalyzers on children under the age of sixteen, marriage courses, and critical remarks about porn parties and violent computer games. The State as moral authority had seemed impossible for centuries in open-minded and tolerant Holland. Now it turned out to be not entirely impossible (and also often not unreasonable).

These examples may seem like haphazard normative interventions, but they were in fact the result of a shift in the national mindset over the years. During previous decades both the left and the right had advocated a shift to more authority and coercion (Vuysje, 1989). In general, a plea for a cultural offensive could be heard (Van den Brink, 2004a). Although the politics of norms and values seemed a failure, this new patronizing attitude did not simply appear out of thin air.[3] A strong moralizing tendency is not unique to the Netherlands (e.g., the "culture wars" in the United States), although it does have Dutch characteristics. In this chapter I analyze the communitarianism of Balkenende (and Etzioni) and the cultural criticism of Dalrymple, and evaluate them in light of the international discussion on conservatism.

The burden of behavior

During the "purple" 1990s in Dutch politics, the think tank of the Christian Democrats laid the foundations of a new agenda for the nation. "Communitarianism" played a major role in that agenda, in particular the ideas of American sociologist Amitai Etzioni, whose book *The New Golden Rule* (1998) was translated and published in Dutch in 2005, with a foreword by Balkenende. According to the Dutch prime minister, Etzioni had written a "communitarian standard work." He emphasized Etzioni's "golden rule," that one should support and respect society's moral order, "just like you want society to respect and support your autonomy" (p. ix).

This somewhat vague "if you scratch my back, then I'll scratch yours" formulation was fleshed out in the book. Etzioni compares his golden rule to the libertarian opinion, in which the free rein of individual freedom ultimately creates the best society. However, he does not embrace the conservative viewpoint that the individual should subordinate him/herself to the community (e.g., Macintyre, 1981). For Etzioni, it is about "the primacy of the social order" (p. 27). Etzioni searches for a middle way and defines communitarianism as the idea that individual freedom is only possible within social cohesion. When viewed from this perspective, every government policy can be interpreted along the lines of Etzioni's communitarianism (even Tony Blair, for example, embraced Etzioni's ideas).

A strong community balanced between individual rights and a regulating state – that is Etzioni's ideal society. He notes that in the West the balance tends more toward autonomy, although he regards "regeneration of the moral order" as possible. But morality is a matter for the communities and thus cannot be imposed. That supposes much dialogue, a vast amount of dialogue. Legislation and regulation can provide nothing more than a starting point or a framework that is the expression of a shared idea which one willingly approves and accepts. In other words, there should be a close relationship between law and morality. The constitutionally given freedom of expression, according to Etzioni, should remain within the norms of civility and decency.

Balkenende's introduction to Etzioni's book (and their personal relationship) leads one to believe that Balkenende wanted to implement a communitarian program, but clearly he did not succeed. Why did that fail, while there was talk of a strong restorative tendency? Theoretically there are three reasons for this. First, resistance from members of the right-wing libertarian VVD party in the first three cabinets was too great. Second, the project was snowed under by major reforms such as privatization of healthcare, reform of the social security laws, participation in the Iraq and Afghanistan wars, integration and assimilation, and security issues. Finally, Balkenende seemed to lack the necessary charisma to make this project appealing.

All three reasons seem plausible. To further examine what happened, it is useful to look at a central component of that project – the WRR report on norms, values, and "the burden of behavior" (2003). On June 9, 2004 the WRR organized a meeting to close the "norms and values project." If I have understood the project leader Kees Schuyt correctly, that should have been the end of the morality debate. The project had been born in the offices of the Christian Democrats during the "purple" cabinets ("as an initiative of an excluded party"). It was pushed through thanks to support from the LPF party.[4] During Balkenende II it was off to a flying start, even though it still had the perceptible scent of its Christian Democrat and LPF origins. Schuyt did not seem to regard a sequel as an obvious next step.

This has all the earmarks of a self-fulfilling prophecy.[5] The WRR's starting point had been pluralism of values, and that should have been the end of it. The report's thesis was that values do not determine behavior. Values are abstract, and they create the space in which behavior takes place. Norms do act as constraints, yet behavior has countless other underlying factors. Thus norms and values are not that important. The council did distinguish a scale of objectionable behaviors (unpleasant, unacceptable, unbearable, and unlawful). According to the WRR, norms and values should be maintained by good example, especially in parenting and education. If pluralism is the ideal, then lack of agreement is not a problem. But if lack of agreement is a problem, then the WRR regards it as a behavioral problem, and not a moral one. The report's rather laborious title, *Values, norms, and the burden of behavior*, underlines this vision.

According to the WRR, the problem was not with the norms and values, but with their compliance. The crux of the problem lies in the transmission of behavioral guidelines and their enforcement through law. For this reason the council argues for more stringent enforcement by government. For the rest, one hopes the normative powers of institutions will suffice, although the council does not mention mobilizing them. Government must be careful not to get involved in disseminating morality, which is always in conflict with the government's role as protector of pluralist values. Put in those terms, that meant the end of Balkenende's crusade. "Values and norms don't fit on a banner" – that opening sentence of the WRR report summed it all up. The cabinet's reaction followed on March 5, 2004 (Ministerie van Algemene Zaken, 2004).

Along with plurality, the importance of "common values" was emphasized. Such values cannot be separated from Dutch history and culture, and are anchored in the Dutch Constitution, with words such as respect, empathy, tolerance, equality, integrity, and sense of responsibility. The cabinet's reaction to norms is that they concern "the boundaries we impose on ourselves." The position of the family – as well as that of the schools – is given special emphasis. Finally, the "role of the government" is set forth in terms of maintaining and actively proclaiming the democratic rule of law, integrity, and the virtues of active citizenship. This initiative was snuffed out like a candle in the wind, not having produced even a single new policy proposal.

A prime minister's impotence

Could the norms-and-values debate possibly have ended differently? The WRR report had neutralized the issue by making behavior the central point, and then emphasizing behavior's multicausal nature. Put in more common terms, the WRR analysis basically came down to the following: Some citizens just don't care, because of lax government enforcement, but that is all government can do. This should be improved, and for the rest we should trust in the institutions. Yet law enforcement indicates that now the problem is too little compliance (see, e.g., Barkhuysen et al., 2005). And what should happen with the "burden of behavior" when there is no legal justification for intervention? And how are institutions supposed to elevate, in a moral sense?

For an effectively functioning legal system, there needs to be some cohesion between "what I approve of, what I shouldn't do, how I should behave, and what others who are relevant think." Plurality of values becomes a problem when there is no moral foundation for compliance with the law. Gabriël van den Brink wrote a background study for the WRR report, boldly entitled *Sketch of a cultural offensive* (2004a), in which he goes much further. His starting point is that a pluralistic, dynamic society needs a certain amount of "normality." According to him, this need not be imposed from above; it can be simply deduced by what citizens consider to be more or less normal.[6]

Van den Brink borrows from the biologist Canquilhem the vision that norms ultimately arise from life itself. There is a normative standard built into every vital behavior. This does not mean that normality is static; human normativity diverges and converges around an average. According to Van den Brink, a cultural offensive comes into being by increasing "the potential and willingness to take into account other individuals in the various areas of life." To explain this requirement of modern citizenship, he uses the metaphor of the highway. One enjoys the individualized freedom of the car while driving, yet one should also abide by the rules, maintain the average speed (and, I would like to add, suffer Holland's notorious traffic jams).

The growing upper middle class is the chosen engine for the cultural offensive. Van den Brink is an unparalleled systems architect who has taken everything into consideration.[7] Even the Dutch royal family shines with potential: "Why don't we take a totally different tack with the royal family, and give it a central role in promoting citizenship!" Van den Brink argues for a kind of moral plan in which the collective is taken into consideration. That means limiting individual freedom to the equivalent of an atomistic auto race. Meanwhile the dilemma of the cultural "defensive" has become crystal clear, and with it Balkenende's impotence.

The WRR embraced pluralism of values as well as any negative consequences from the resulting individualization. Maintaining legal standards and correcting excesses were finished with; there was nothing more for the government to do. Institutions would take care of the rest. In contrast, Van den Brink argues for placing a brake on individualization through substantial normative demands on citizens that "the collective" can sustain. He then drives the very hook that was removed from the discussion by the WRR even deeper. That the government has nothing but a procedural role, as the WRR formulates it, cannot have been Balkenende's position.

And yet Balkenende cannot go as far as Van den Brink proposes. A vigorous campaign to propagate normative principles was probably asking too much of his European-style libertarian coalition partners. It would be easier (but still quite a challenge) for the government to establish a normative position at the legal level: security (the subject of the next chapter). Balkenende's first cabinet – which lasted only eight months – produced only one policy plan: *Toward a safer society.*[8] In other words, Balkenende was politically and conceptually unable to give the moral offensive more substance. Etzioni's starting points remain too general for a politically profiled position; the WRR did not produce sufficient direction and ammunition for government policy; and positions such as Van den Brink's are not really feasible in a modern, socially liberal society. After that, little remained of the proposed moral strengthening of civil society. Balkenende had sufficient political support only in his fourth (or nanny) cabinet, but that resulted in nothing more than bungling.

Dalrymple the gadfly

Besides the communitarian moralism of Balkenende, the preceding decade also saw the rise of the cultural conservatism of social critic Theodore Dalrymple and his philosophical counterpart Roger Scruton (for example, 2007). During the last few years, Dalrymple in particular could depend on a warm welcome in the Netherlands. He was invited to speak at prestigious conferences, visited various branches of government, and was often published in both newspaper sections and weeklies. He was appreciated throughout the Netherlands as a gadfly[9] who brought his "inconvenient truth." His real name, however, is Anthony Daniels, and his truth was not what it was cracked up to be. Nevertheless, Dalrymple was a hit in

Balkenende's Netherlands. Even though (according to him) he was ignored in his own land, the Dutch could not get enough of him.[10]

Dalrymple's vision is an all too common story. Civilization had been squandered by the 1960s generation, which destroyed everything of value, except itself. In *Life at the Bottom* Dalrymple shows how this mentality supported an underclass, or even created one. Instead of being given incentives to achieve something in life, they were shown how they were victims of their conditions. We were too soft on this underclass and, as a result, have undermined civilization. Or perhaps the opposite is better: we have destroyed our civilization and, as a result, have created an underclass! "In fact, most of the social pathology exhibited by the underclass has its origins in ideas that have filtered down from the intelligentsia" (2001, p. x).

Dalrymple claims his authority to speak on this subject from his psychiatric work with junkies, alcoholics, whores, and criminals. He claims to have seen 10,000 persons in a period of ten years, "lives dominated, almost without exception, by violence, crime, and degradation" (p. vii). Not counting the weekends, that comes out to seeing four unique cases a day (in a hospital and a prison). Dalrymple has a flair for hyperbole, which lends his work a gloss of enormous power. "But in nine-tenths of the cases (in my experience) the distress is self-inflicted or at least the consequence of not knowing how to live" (about junkies, p. 24).

Notice the difference between "self-inflicted" and "not knowing how to live" in that quotation. Dalrymple bridges this gap by referring to the emptiness in society. In *Our culture, what's left of it* (2005), he serves up with great relish the apparitions of a lost civilization. The decay has deep roots. Virginia Woolf and D.H. Lawrence were among the early gravediggers. Huxley's *Brave new world* (1932) and Orwell's *1984* (1949) were clarion blasts: both dystopias seem to have been prophetic, "almost in a biblical sense" (2005, p. 130). Apparently civilization was vulnerable, and recent decades have culminated in the final destruction. Punk music and tattoos flourish – thanks to cultural relativism – and have achieved cultural prominence.

Without real cultural challenge, entertainment and relationships are all that is left. Entertainment has degenerated, and personal relationships (without commitments) are "purely instrumental" in this era. There is a direct line between the downfall of civilization and the creation of an underclass – the stimulus for the individual to take action is missing. Cultural relativism leads to degeneration and self-chosen victimhood. That message resonates throughout almost every page of his work. It is tempting to pile up citation after citation. Dalrymple writes as one possessed, and his sketches of the bottom of society are heart rending, poisonous, and vengeful, but ultimately his analyses are too thin to hold water.

Dalrymple's most important proposal for how things can be different is to be found in a moral address to people about their own deeds and their own lives. That is an important but limited cue. The cultural changes are too great to turn back with a simple flip of a morality switch. Those who are acquainted with the normative wrestling of many professionals (see, e.g., Tonkens et al., 2006b) understand the shortcomings of Dalrymple's position. Viewed politically, Dalrymple's answer is ultimately that of Hayek and neoliberal thinkers. "The British . . . are still attached to their state as calves to the udder" (2005, p. 200).[11] His criticism leads logically to reducing the size of government and its affiliated institutions.

Less government and more self-responsibility on the part of citizens is the motto. "Social responsibility, no state control" is the slogan of the Scottish Conservative Party. Therein lies the difference between Dalrymple and Etzioni. However, less government inevitably leads to more market, which – even for Dalrymple – can largely be held responsible for the subversion of civilization he describes. The years under Balkenende have shown that moral rearmament (norms and values) cannot stand up to the turbulent forces of a globalizing economy. Carping on the loss of civilization is irrelevant if the new context is not understood and taken into account.[12]

The conservative turn

Balkenende's failed crusade and Dalrymple's success were part of what can be considered a right-wing conservative turn. The conservative era has arrived, rejoices historian Bart Jan Spruyt[13] in the epilogue of *In praise of conservatism* (2003 in Dutch, p. 204). Given the history of Dutch politics, that was a bold statement; during the entire twentieth century only a handful have taken this position. Spruyt listed the columnist Heldring and historians Huizinga, Van Deursen, and Kossmann. Those were the Dutch Mohicans of conservative thought (followed by the trio of law philosophers in Leiden: Paul Cliteur, Andreas Kinneging, and Ashfin Ellian). But what does that conservative moment consist of?

It is not difficult to point out the conflicts and inconsistencies that are covered by the label "conservative." Tanenhaus (2009) makes an enlightening distinction between the traditionally prudent (American) conservatism of Edmund Burke (1730-1797) and the aggressive "radical revanchism" of former president George W. Bush and the Tea Party. According to Tanenhaus, classical conservatism went under in the 1970s (hence the title of his book, *The death of conservatism*). Let me focus on that traditional conservatism for a moment.[14]

This traditional line of thought has its origin in the Enlightenment, as did socialism and liberalism, and in particular in the aversion to the French Revolution of 1789. In a nutshell, for socialists the revolution meant the dawn of even further reforms, for liberals the end result of history, and for conservatives the horror of the people's power. The fall of the aristocracy, the overestimation of reason, and the rejection of traditions were viewed by, e.g., Edmund Burke and Alexis de Toqueville (1805-1859) as enormous errors with regard to what they considered the natural order.

Natural order points, first and foremost, to the conflict – and its historical results – between human evil and disciplining via the institutions of the family, the church, and lastly the state. The moral shortcomings of humankind can be regarded as the fundamental doctrine of conservatism. Insofar as one can speak of "the good," it should be realized with great effort, focus, and concentration. The formation of conscience, building of character, rearing to virtue represent the hope of the – generally rather somber – conservatives.

Self-control – resulting from force, external pressure, and practice – is a basic theme in conservative thought, hence the importance given to community and family ties. Repression, social control, and formation of conscience form a triangle that is regarded as necessary for a civilized coexistence. At its core, conservatism is a cultural and pedagogical ideal – at least according to Spruyt (2003, p. 11) – and only secondarily a constitutional and political concept. As a political movement, conservatism is focused on societal stability and the need for cultural continuity and it seeks this mainly in the institutions that humans have been given from nature: the family, religion, tribal bonds, the community, and the traditions that give them their form.

These are exactly the institutions that have suffered a considerable setback in modern times. The emancipation of the individual and the superiority of the modern state – propelled, respectively by liberalism and socialism – have specifically undermined these "self-evident" achievements of human history. The individual has been put on the throne and the doctrine of moral virtue has been transformed into a procedural ethics with no immanent direction. If no higher order is recognized – God, Nature, Society – then in principle anything is possible, and as a consequence nothing is possible. "What remains if reason no longer clings to the old morality are the purely natural ideals that were cherished by the cave dweller – wealth, power, security," according to Van Deursen in his 1994 Huizinga lecture (quoted by Spruyt, 2003, p. 184).

Wealth, power, and security – these are the key terms of an advanced modern society. In his book's epilogue, Spruyt (p. 199) points out that there are no political blueprints for conservatism. Insofar as one can speak of a movement, it is first and foremost a cultural program, in which "there must be an end to the cultivation of naïve innocence. Adult values must again be honored – realism, responsibility, and the absence of illusions." It seems that the political translation of this cultural ideal has meant the demise of the Edmund Burke Society and with it the classical conservative movement in the Netherlands.[15]

The relevance of conservatism

In contemporary times, there seem to be no illusions left, and this suits Spruyt perfectly. Bauman, among others, sees the postmodern era as modernity without illusions (1993). The twentieth century had been characterized by ideological conflict in which pacification had blossomed profusely. With World War II as a moral anchor point and the Soviet Union as a frightening counterpoint, a relative consensus developed around striving for freedom, equality, and fraternity. September 11 brought a definitive end to the reasonably successful second half of the twentieth century. The "social perspective," defined as belief in the goodness of humanity under proper societal conditions, was common during the postwar period. It seemed to be the answer to Auschwitz and the Gulag.

This idealistic perspective laid the foundation for the development of welfare states in the West. In the Netherlands, shifting coalitions of social democratic solidarity, Christian democratic brotherly love, and free-market thinking achieved unprecedented successes. This allowed plenty of space for the emancipation of the individual, it led to the growth of the middle class, and it even offered possibilities for international solidarity. There was almost no room left for criticism of the Enlightenment, the ideals of the French Revolution, and just as little for appreciation of traditions. Conservative thinking – insofar as one spoke of it – could be regarded as something for grumpy old men.

This situation has changed drastically. There is a vast range of problems for which the said "social perspective" has no answer. Mass migrations, terrorism, criminality, moral unease, and climate change form a grim and dramatic list of issues over which it is impossible to have any illusions. It has also become philosophically fashionable to warn of overwrought ideals (Gray, 2007; Achterhuis, 1998, 2008). Yet this turn seems more like a turning away from the social ideal that was the main theme for so long and in so many variations.

Even though the social perspective had established itself quite comfortably, social democracy became the favorite target of conservative thinkers. Christian democracy can always boast of its religiously moral ideology, and European liberalism stands on its "mature values" of realism, responsibility, and lack of illusions. Conservatives projected the inclination to evil on human existence, whereas socialism at its core was based on fighting the evil of society. Expressions of individual wickedness are again and again a slap in the face of the gullible socialist. Misuse of social services, deceitful tales told by asylum seekers, random forms of violence – these are unacceptable for both the social being and the societal image, and in a certain sense even seem unimaginable.

In contrast, conservatives point to the ambivalence between individual empowerment and the tendency to evil, according to Andreas Kinneging (2000). The first strengthens the second. He finds that social thinking dominates society, and he holds the social sciences responsible for this. They obscure the insights of wisdom, sensibility, and virtue.[16] Instead of the community, now the government has the role of curbing negative passions. "Enlightenment thinking, in other words, has turned man into a heavily armed barbarian, a being who controls everything except himself." It seems that the "conservative moment" appeared when emancipation of the individual began to show its worst side. All this was set against a backdrop of terrorism, an unstoppable flood of immigrants, and "the little civil war" (Enzensberger, 1992).

In such a world without illusions, conservatism seems to be one of the few more or less coherent views of humankind and society. This is not because it formulates a new illusion, but precisely because it defines or redefines existing relationships, cultural traditions, and "what is normal." As a "cultural-pedagogical" ideal, conservatism invites reflection on internal motivations and modes of behavior. It adds an understandable marginal note to the undesirable consequences of the emancipation of the individual. Furthermore, the realism advocated in approaching citizens (rather than "victims") can be fruitful. But what does this mean for the present day?

An outmoded right

In a world without boundaries, there is fertile ground for conservative ideas when it comes to retooling traditions and responsibilities for a new societal context. Yet conservative thinking also harbors an inherent aversion to government taking on social responsibility. For example, Spruyt (2003) argues in his epilogue for the demolition of the healthcare and social welfare branches of the government. They stand in the way of the community's formative function. "The longer the state retains the welfare branches, the smaller the chance that the fabric of the community can restore itself" (p. 209). This presupposes some form of vitality in the community, which for the time being should be regarded as illusory.

It seems the government has a prominent and indispensable role to play in the social vitality of the actual, dynamic community. Faith in the restoration of lost communal ties is naïve and illusory. In any event, the Dutch cultural offensive described earlier in this chapter resulted in extreme governmental interference in social life. The precarious social ties of the networked society are being increasingly supported by government (for example, with social intervention teams). This kind of bureaucratic meddling shapes the translation of the conservative moment, which could not form a political-cultural movement within the Dutch tradition.

The moral policies of the Dutch government in the twentieth century were the result of the so called "pillarizaton" of society. Laws and regulations could boast of reflecting the neatly organized ideological pillars of the Dutch social order. This in turn led to the deeply rooted conviction that the state should not act independently with regard to moral questions. The WRR report (2004) argued for an institutional approach. Schools, healthcare and social services, and youth services should carry the "burden of behavior." Yet these institutions lack the ideological sustenance of the pillars from which they stem. Hope is placed in the institutions, but where do these institutions get *their* hope?

In the absence of a societal tradition, the government seems to have attracted "morality" to itself. The policy is restorative, with various patronizing and authoritarian traits, and with no distinctive ideological embedding. The next chapter shows how it inserted itself via preventive security policies. In the absence of a common conservative tradition, the Dutch government pragmatically picked up the gauntlet, and was supported by a significant part of the population. In his controversial book *What's the matter with Kansas?,* journalist Thomas Frank (2004)[17] shows how the Republicans managed to win over the poor residents of that state by systematically playing moral trump cards – abortion, same-sex marriage, and prayer in the classroom. The "cultural war" dominated over socioeconomic interests.[18]

Frank's analysis of the importance of moral issues has not gone unchallenged,[19] the main criticism being that economic interests are indeed important. In a detailed analysis of speeches and campaign material, Smith (2007) shows how the "jobs and growth" narrative was told, and that the Republicans' success ultimately came from a rhetorical reframing of economic interests.[20] Be that as it may, it seems justified to also interpret the Dutch cultural offensive as a combination of conservative sociocultural sentiments and European liberal socioeconomic policy. One can point to the high costs of the welfare state and the influx of foreigners into lower-class neighborhoods. Conservatism becomes a reservoir for the rage described in the previous chapter.

The cultural changes in the world without boundaries cannot easily be undone. Economically and socially, we are dealing with a totally different world. Belief in the restoration of an orderly world becomes outdated when the new conditions are not understood and taken into account. How can a culture that has been severely shaken up by globalization and individualization reorganize itself in an appealing way? That is the political challenge of the coming years. The conservative criticism of culture should hold up a sharply revealing mirror, yet that could quickly begin to display signs of authoritarian policy. That in turn feeds the rage from frustrated *thymos* described in the previous chapter, and as such is the carrier of populism.

Actual normative policy is characterized by a restrictive approach. The cultural offensive was inserted in the security policy that took shape in the mid-1990s.[21] Before going on to the next chapter, let me note that the difference between repressive and preventive policies is gradually losing its significance. Repressive policies have increasingly become more preventive in nature, and are often enacted "proactively." On the other hand, preventive actions are often so radically restrictive that they can in fact be called repressive. In the next chapter I look at the second program for ordering, which belongs to law enforcement and security. This is an area where the state has traditionally had legitimate authority.

CHAPTER 4

SAFE NEW WORLD

From time to time I track the number of minutes devoted to security-related topics on the national news. Often it amounts to more than half of the broadcast time available. There was an attempted terrorist attack somewhere, an escapee from an asylum, or a suspected dealer in child pornography is being extradited. But this kind of impressionistic research soon gets tangled up in definitions. Should I include accidents – perhaps those caused by carelessness? – or disasters – a guilty party is soon found, or possibly the first responders arrived late? Or take the discussion about norms and values: it is easy to argue that they are related to questions of security. And I haven't even mentioned food safety, or – something totally different – the social safety net provided by the government (e.g., unemployment benefits).

Security, in other words, deals with anything and everything – and hence nothing, according to current opinion. Yet I dare to doubt that last. The fact that all these subjects can be placed within the framework of security says a great deal about our society. One way or another, security always seems to be the solution. We address a lot of problems when we use it as an argument – cameras, child records, license plate recognition, body scans. I have called the concept of security a semantic dragnet in a liquid society (Boutellier, 2005). It ranges from dog poop to terrorism and from child molesters to trash in the streets. And that is just "social safety," or safety related to human behavior.[1]

When speaking of criminality, words such as "crime" and "punishment" sound almost old-fashioned. Just as the motto "law and order" seemed outdated in the 1970s, "guilt and penance" smacks of Moscow in the nineteenth century. Old-fashioned and yet timeless, crime, punishment, law, order, guilt, and penance have obviously not disappeared from the conceptual stage. But these words no longer define thought and action in the area of "what is wrong and what you can do about it." In the 1990s, criminality became a risk, and punishment was one option within a much larger arsenal of instruments of control. The discourse about criminality was moved from "crime and punishment" to "risk and control," and sometimes to the even vaguer "insecurity and precaution." Security has taken conceptual control of moral space and thus has taken on an ordering quality.[2]

A new mission for criminal justice

I begin my conceptual reconnaissance with punishment. One does not need to argue that the criminal justice system enjoys a great deal of attention. There is even a large conglomerate of critical researchers, television producers, and journalists holding the public prosecutors' and the judges' feet to the fire. This attention has a paradoxical cause – expectations are highly charged, and this promotes mistrust. One wonders about both the effectiveness of criminal law (many citizens want more and stronger sentences) and the reliability of the verdicts. Indignation over procedural mistakes alternates with protests about judgments in dubious cases. Criminal justice itself seems to have become a societal "hanging offense." I will return to this in Chapter 7; at present I am concerned with the meaning accorded to punishments.

Among others, the criminologist David Garland (2001) regards the renewed appreciation for sentencing as one of the hallmarks of the current "culture of control." What is the nature of this "new faith" in the criminal justice system, which is determined more by its pretensions than its actual performance? The function of criminal justice is regarded in general as a channeling of revenge into a proportionally acceptable retribution for the deed. Utilitarian goals are also added to the punishment, such as compensation, deterrence, prevention, and rehabilitation. Restrained punishments – and trying to make the best of them – could be an official "civilizing mission statement" for criminal law.

There is also a psychological tendency to punish. As Van Ruller (1993, p. 346) describes it, "the punitive need comes . . . from a spontaneous impulse that can be calmed by sanctions." Adam Smith spoke of spontaneous resentment, Nietzsche of a primal human impulse, Durkheim of spontaneous indignation, and Garland of penality (a somewhat difficult-to-explain concept that also includes the emotional aspects of punishment). Van Ruller regards this punitive impulse as emotional, and hence irrational. This punitive drive has been rediscovered in recent decades, or perhaps I should say that it has found a renewed appreciation.

To understand this renewed appreciation, I think it is important not to speak of an "irrational impulse." In fact, it is a deliberately conscious choice *for* punishment that I would describe as a counter to forbearance toward criminal behavior. It is the avenging *thymos* that was discussed in Chapter 2. It is about a deliberate rejection of punishable behavior and an express will to make the offender suffer. It is not just about a need for retribution, but also the belief that society needs such a "normative justice."

Let me illustrate this proposition with a citation from Gerrit Krol's novel *De vitalist.*[3] A discussion about punishment takes place after a murder: *"We good citizens are no longer capable of paying back in kind, not technically and not morally. Not through personal initiative." "What are you saying?" "Dammit, listen to me. I say, if you need to, feel ashamed of doing it, but do it. Punish. Dare to punish. That's better than holding back. And letting the murderers walk away."* (Krol, 2000, p. 114f.). Krol is not talking about the need to punish, but rather about the aversion to punishing, which he rejects: "Dare to punish." He points to the necessity of reciprocating evil with evil and the courage required to do just that.

This "rationality" in the punitive motive is a reaction to the long stretch of history in which the avenging motive was kept in abeyance. For several centuries the perpetrator could count on increasing compassion. In his extensive study of two hundred years of Dutch prison life, Herman Franke explains this through the growing power of suffering:[4] "From contemptible, almost bestial creatures who died of hunger and misery in poorly-heated, unhygienic hovels and underground holes, Dutch prisoners have become reasonably well-housed detainees" (Franke, 2005, p. 4). He points to the growing distaste for physical violence and cruelty, and describes this tendency, inspired by the work of Norbert Elias, as the result of a historical civilizing process. That same aversion was occurring throughout western societies.

The rise of nation-states and the growth of their interdependence led to a different psychological mindset in which the role of physical violence became marginalized.[5] Up to the beginning of the nineteenth century, many criminals were drawn and quartered, with loud encouragement from the public. Then punishment began to lose its sharper edges, alternatives were found, reintegration programs were introduced, and there was more tolerance and exoneration. The power of suffering grew so strong that it apparently compromised another motive – the will to punish.

The criminal justice system tacks back and forth between the two impulses of vengeance and compassion. The system should be well balanced with regard to the punitive impulse, as well as the tendency to lenience. One needs little evidence that currently the second impulse dominates, namely in an instrumental sense – we punish to keep society orderly. During previous decades "the emancipation of prisoners" came to an end.[6] Although this shift in compassion for the criminal had set in earlier in the Netherlands,[7] it seems that the white paper "Toward a safer society" (*Naar een veiliger samenleving*, 2002) marked the definitive break with the emancipation of prisoners. The white paper is a vast porridge of regulations to the tune of "more, harder, and more effective,"[8] which attests to a strong belief in vindictive normativity. Leaving crime unpunished, according to this attitude, ultimately devalues modern society's level of civilization – a shift in meaning that has found much resonance in society.

From criminality to insecurity

Renewed faith in punishment is a crucial step in reconstructing the process by which security grew into a program for ordering. In a pluralistic culture, crime is increasingly regarded as a choice for which one should be held accountable. In a complex world without direction, criminal law now functions as an orientation point, and that changes the meaning of punishment. The number of judgments has increased, punishments are more severe, and in general the approach to dealing with criminality, nuisance, and antisocial behavior has become tougher. But this is only a part of the story; attention to crime prevention has also grown. This development has been discussed often (see, e.g., Van Dijk & De Waard, 2009), so I shall not repeat it here. My concern here is with the relation between the new criminal justice mission and the prevention perspective.

There are two strategies for tackling problems – correction and prevention. This also applies to problems of criminality. In the first instance one speaks of a legal reaction (repression); in the second, steps are taken to avoid offensive behavior (prevention). And yet the contrast between repression and prevention in practice is not as sharp as is often thought. Punishment is composed of various goals, including the goal of preventing offensive behavior in the future. And so, vice versa, a prevention policy also entails some form of correction. It seems to me that the attempt to bring both under one label contributed to the rise in popularity of the concept of security.

As a concept, security makes the relation between the "repression" reaction and the "prevention" vanguard possible. Use of the concept of security in the Netherlands is a fairly recent phenomenon. In 1993 the Dutch Ministry of the Interior published the first Security and Safety Report (*Integrale veiligheidsrapportage*). In hindsight that was a meaningful moment in the history of crime-fighting (Cachet & Ringeling, 2005). By redefining criminality as insecurity, three bridges were created – from factual offense to the risk thereof; from enforcement of criminal law to other measures; and from objective events to their subjective experience.[9] These three bridges made it possible to link together the two strategies of repression and prevention.

From fact to risk

The first bridge brings crime into the category of risk, along with many other risks, e.g., fires, disasters, terrorism, and major hazardous materials accidents. One hoped, with an integrated and comprehensive safety policy, to bring more consistency into local approaches to safety problems, but that was never a huge success (Cachet & Ringeling, 2005). Policy makers apparently misjudged the complexity of the field. Besides, criminality has a moral angle that goads both the public and politicians into indignation and action. Even more important than the actual connection of various forms of security was the shift in thinking in terms of risk analysis and risk management. Criminality has a potentially negative effect, and so it winds up on the agenda of the risk society.

That is an important fact. Risk is regarded by various authors as the key word of the twenty-first century. Ulrich Beck coined the term "risk society" in 1986 with regard to technological developments (e.g., nuclear power and genetic engineering), but the idea's penetration into other fields has proved to be even more important. Furedi (1997, p. xii), for example, shows that use of the word "risk" in papers published in English rose from 2,037 in 1994 to 18,003 in 2000. In that same year, actuarial researcher Ewald described risk as "the single point upon which contemporary societies question themselves, analyse themselves, seek their values and perhaps recognize their limits" (quoted by Ericson, 2007, p. 6). According to audit expert Michael Power (2007), risk is *the* organizing concept in an uncertain world.

Power (2004) had written earlier about "the risk management of everything." And so criminality also becomes "a risk." This shift in meaning fits perfectly with the tendency to try to avoid criminality (instead of waiting until suffering has occurred). As early as 1985 it had been noted that police and the judicial system fell short in their capacity and responsibilities to stem the increase in crime (*Samenleving en criminaliteit*, 1985). By redefining crime as "risk," all kinds of new techniques became possible, which were developed in the insurance industry, among others. This is why Feeley and Simon (1994) speak of "actuarial justice" and Van Swaaningen (1996) of "risk justice." These characterizations, however, miss the point – it is not so much the judiciary as the other organizations that are responsible for risk management.

At present one notes that preventive thinking is being assimilated into the emerging concept of "precaution." This concept, which drifted over from environmental law, is about government not waiting for scientific certainty before taking action in the event of potentially serious damage (Fischer, 2001; quoted in Ericson, 2007, p. 21). The *chance* of damage is sufficient justification, even in the absence of calculable risk.[10] It is tempting to characterize thinking about security in this vein as precautionary politics (Ericson, 2007, tends in this direction; for the Netherlands, see Pieterman, 2008). I will return to this later in this chapter, but for now it will suffice to refer to the semantic shift from criminal fact to risk of damage.

From reaction to regulation

The second bridge, which is between criminal law and administrative regulation, makes municipalities and other organizations co-responsible for security problems. Crime is defined in the penal code, and the government, police, and judicial system have a legal responsibility to fight it. For the police, this judicial task is supplemented with maintaining order locally and helping in crisis situations. When this task is defined as a security problem, with an emphasis on risk analysis and risk management, then many more parties can become involved in prevention and repression, as well as remediation. Garland (1996, 2001) has described this process, in which other parties are made responsible for security issues, as *responsibilization*.

Now the question is whether this "intrusive" characterization is really accurate. Municipalities, schools, and Dutch housing corporations have their own initiatives regarding security issues. As a result, the field of security has expanded enormously, and this led to a new problem – the need for all involved to coordinate and collaborate. The talk now is of safety networks (Terpstra & Kouwenhoven, 2004; Boutellier, 2005). It was in reference to this that I proposed a "line" model – as in soccer – in which the various societal functions of the community are presented in terms of defense (repression), center field (norms), and forward line (vitality) (Boutellier, 2005; Boutellier & Van Steden, 2010).

The judiciary and the police have traditionally played a peripheral role in maintaining social order. In their current position, their normative function gives direction to other social institutions. This is one reason Simon (2007), for example, speaks of "governing through crime." According to him (p. 4f.), there are three strategies at work: crime-fighting per se (3 percent of adults in the United States are in some form of detention or under supervision); using crime to legitimize other goals (e.g., dealing with "anti-social families"); and the influence of technologies, narratives, and metaphors about criminality in other public institutions (e.g., school safety).

For example, although only one in ten American schools has to deal with violence, all American schools have prevention programs and disciplinary procedures (p. 213). Simon even speaks of a punitive pedagogy (p. 220) of uniforms, zero-tolerance policies, and lockdowns. The dramatic situation sketched by Simon is not applicable to the Dutch situation.[11] Disciplinary techniques such as school uniforms and lockdowns are more or less unthinkable in Dutch society. In contrast, one can point to Dutch school safety policy and the increasing practice of family intervention. I see these initiatives more as an attempt to "remoralize," along the lines of the cultural offensive discussed in the previous chapter, rather than "governing through crime."

From facts to feelings

The third bridge is between the objective crime and the subjective experience of the situation. Something happens in a criminal event. There is a concrete experience, and one reacts. "Safe" or "unsafe," however, refers to a feeling, which is relatively independent of the actual situation. For that reason alone, the concept of safety cannot be defined in an objective sense (e.g., Roels, 2005; Zedner, 2009). When can one talk about actual safety? Yet "how the citizen feels" does legitimize the idea of security. Even if a citizen has never been the victim of a crime, feelings of insecurity can still exist. In turn, even though no crook is caught, it can feel safer if, for example, there is more surveillance.

The subjective experience of security is a remarkably complicated business. Elffers and De Jong (2004) showed in qualitative research that residents in problem areas regard "unsafety" as a synonym for social problems. Crude behavior, indecency, littering and pollution, noise, aggressive driving, and "those foreigners" are the residents' primary complaints. Research shows that there are four layers in the fear of crime: fear of actually becoming a victim of crime; the unease surrounding crime as a social problem; dissatisfaction with other social problems; and general discontent with today's society.[12]

It is also possible to view these negative factors from a more positive angle. In Amsterdam, the Research and Statistics office (in collaboration with the academic chair for Security and Citizenship) researched "trust in the neighborhood" and "social cohesion" as determinants in fear of crime. They appeared to be just as influential as experiences of having been a victim (Boers et al., 2008). Etymologically, the Dutch word for "security" – *veiligheid* – also encompasses shelter, intimacy, safety, and comfort (Van Zuijlen, 2004). As such, the pursuit of security can be seen as a synonym for social policy, which is all-encompassing.

The moral inversion

Viewed from the concept of security, the problem of criminality thus becomes broader in a material sense, more diverse in an administrative sense, and deeper in a psychological sense. This has resulted in a larger movement with more resources, more strategies and methods, and more relevant actors. Statistics Netherlands calculated that expenditures on security policy rose an average of 6 percent per annum between 2002 and 2009.[13]

The new civilizing mission of the criminal justice system – no tolerance for antisocial behavior – has spread to other policy areas, thanks to the broadening concept of security. This has major consequences for the nature of government intervention.

In the classical paradigm, intervention by the criminal justice system is *in* the last instance *the* last instance. This idea presupposes a strong civil community that achieves social ordering through socialization, inculcation of norms and values, and social control. If civil discipline is not sufficient, the sanctioning system moves from the periphery to the center of society. It occupies moral space, but, being a judicial instrument, it cannot fill it. The concept of "security" offers relief. It reverses the relationship between the social order and the criminal justice system, which no longer simply guards the borders of moral space, but also lays claim to its internal arrangement. This is not a matter of normative broadening, but rather of a reversal. I would call it a moral inversion.[14]

An enlightening illustration is the approach to antisocial behavior in England and Wales. Frank Field, a Labour Member of Parliament, describes the need for a "politics of behavior" in his chillingly titled book, *Neighbours from hell* (2003). Field's opinion is that a certain degree of respect and civility are necessary for a well-functioning society. To that end, good behavior should be encouraged and bad behavior rejected. The old structures for doing that, however, have eroded. Faith (in this case religion) has changed into permanent doubt and a pervasive relativism has permeated institutions such as the family and the education system: "my views are just as good as yours" (Field, 2003, p. 3). So far Field's narrative sounds familiar – it echoes Dalrymple.

In contrast to Dalrymple, Field wants to see action on the part of the government: "the use of the law has to be backed up by a strategy to teach again all of those social virtues" (p. 23). In his view the most important virtues are courtesy, consideration, and sensitivity to others. Addressing antisocial behavior is therefore important, because it is the frequency of the disturbance that is the decisive factor – it makes rancor understandable.[15] Criminal justice falls short in this regard – it takes too long, there are too few funds, and "the law favours the perpetrator" (p. 35f.). Field regards a rigorous approach by the government as legitimate because politics is about more than managing the market. The question "what kind of people do we want to be" is also political (p. 50). Because of this conviction he sees the police as a surrogate parent for youths who have gone astray, and he wants the social sector to function more as a "teacher" for young families.

This political barb, according to the criminologist Adam Crawford, has had a great impact on security policies in England and Wales.[16] In particular, Crawford (2009a, 2009b) regards the Anti-Social Behaviour Act of 2003 as a new kind of behavior regulation. An "ASBO" can be imposed by local authorities, and violations can be legally penalized. If someone who has been ordered to stay away from a certain street violates that order, then jail time can be imposed. The ASBO lowers the threshold of intervention, formalizes informal reactions, and intensifies possible sanctions (Crawford, 2009a, p. 813). He is also of the opinion that the ASBO undermines traditional forms of judicial protection – due process, proportionality, and protection of the rights of juveniles.

Because general social policy is less successful, Crawford thinks there is a tendency toward individually-oriented interventions: "prevention in a context of uncertainty" leads to "steering, monitoring and correcting people's lifestyles" (2009a, p. 815). Crawford counts a grand total of 18 instruments of regulation in England and Wales, ranging from the Drug Intervention Order, the Parenting Contract, and Housing Benefit Sanctions, to Drinking Banning Orders and Crack House Closure (p. 8). Blurring the border between punishments and measures may seem like a solution to local authorities, but for many jurists it is a horror (Ashworth & Zedner, 2008). Complaints, powers of imposition, and sanctions all contain arbitrary elements.[17]

Criminal law is not suitable for dealing with social problems, which is why refuge is sought in what we could call "quasi-criminal law" – hence the moral inversion. The Netherlands has far fewer nationally controlled "politics of behavior," although there are more local prohibitions. In 2008, twenty-five communities had active ordinances against public gatherings; there are also ordinances against alcohol and drugs, behavior (e.g., the *FF Kappen* or "Cut it out" program in Rotterdam), and against weapons and the like (Brouwer & Schilder, 2008). These authors concluded that there is a toughening up – via municipal ordinances – of local norms, in nature, content, and sanctions. These ordinances often use vague terminology and their application is not subject to direct democratic control.

Whatever the differences between England and the Netherlands, the difference in insight between Field and Crawford leads us into the heart of the political-moral discussion about security that is being held in almost all Western nations. Does one adopt a pro-active behavioral approach, or a restrained criminal justice reaction? It is crystal clear that "neighbors from hell" and intimidating and disturbing behavior are not pleasant for those who live nearby. It is very problematic, especially from a political standpoint, when government cannot find answers to these situations. On the other hand, citizens' rights to freedom from government intervention have been built up carefully over the centuries and could possibly be destroyed, albeit unintentionally.[18]

The security of everything

Based on the moral inversion described above, there is increasing discussion of the "securitization of society" (originally Waever, 1995). In government buildings, the receptionists of old have been replaced with security guards. Fans are now physically searched before soccer matches, and one can also be asked to show identification on a train platform. Various authors see this "securitization" as the result of the utopian longing in "a world that is no longer utopian" (Loader, 2008, p. 404; see also Boutellier, 2002). Security is beginning to function more like a lens through which to examine social problems. Crime is normal, as is its prevention. In criminology, this translated into the "routine activity approach," which proposes that an offense is the coming together of "a likely offender, a suitable target and the absence of a capable guardian" (Felson, 1998, p. 3).

This delineates the exceptional consequences of the moral inversion. The law begins to function more as a form of congealed morality than as a normative set of coordinates. It gives direction to public morals, which defines "the good life" according to the degree of compliance. Not the content of the norms, but their effectiveness – even better, their enforceability – becomes the goal of the security approach. The norm becomes an (insurable) risk, its transgression an opportunity, and prevention a question of control. Zedner (2007) speaks in this context of a "pre-crime" logic that translates into new technologies and regulations.

So we see the development of surveillance technology (from cameras to body scans; Lyon, 2007), situational crime prevention (regulations around risk situations and risk citizens; Reiner, 2006), community safety (numerous neighborhood security initiatives; Crawford, 2003), individual risk assessment (feminism plays an interesting role in this; e.g., Lünnemann, 2007), insurance technologies (Feeley & Simon, 1994), registries of offenders and other forms of preventive measures and monitoring (the previously mentioned system of "quasi-criminal law"),[19] and preventive detention, each and every one of them new approaches, which according to Zedner (2007) are at odds with the procedural guarantees of the criminal justice process.

"Pre-crime" logic has no boundaries. Before there is even a mention of a definable or calculable risk, there is the possibility of a risk developing. Power writes of "an increasing demand for governance of the unknowable" (quoted by Zedner, 2007, p. 85). In this context, one hears the word "precaution," which goes further than "risk law" when applied to the field of criminal activity. Here a relationship with strategies from international security arises, for example, pre-emptive strikes, anticipatory self-defense, and rapid-fire justice. A quote from former American Secretary of Defense Donald Rumsfeld about this speaks volumes: "There are known knowns. These are things we know that we know. There are known unknowns. That is to say, there are things that we know we don't know. But there are also unknown unknowns. These are things we don't know we don't know" (quoted in Zedner, 2009, p. 126).

Here we find ourselves facing a paradoxical development. We view criminal activity as "a routine activity" (Felson, 1998), as a self-evident aspect of the "high crime culture" (Garland, 1996). And yet this normalization leads to a permanent sense of being threatened. It means that normal people can strike at any time, anywhere. The normalization of "evil" leads to the fear that it can pop up anywhere, at any time. This fundamental distrust opens the door to an unrestrained security offensive, supported by technological possibilities. According to Koops et al. (2009), the modern citizen is becoming a transmitter surrounded by a digital cloud of information. A variety of personalized tracking systems forms around him or her, e.g., electronic medical files, children's files, student tracking systems, Social Security numbers, auto registration and verification of license plate numbers on highways, cameras, internet usage records, electronic pay cards for tolls and fares, GPS usage records, and credit scores.

Each of these has its own objective, yet they all have a more or less explicit security component, certainly "if it comes to that." In the event of serious crimes, no one objects to these sources being used in the investigation, and that rapidly becomes the case with less serious offenses. DNA sampling is a good example. It has been successively permitted on a voluntary basis for serious crimes, then for less serious offenses, and then even without permission and with the possibility that it will be subsequently stored for all citizens in a data bank. This seems to be an application of salami tactics – realizing one's goal with many small steps that obscure the big picture.

The word "tactics" presupposes a conscious and deliberate strategy, yet this process of securitization probably takes place innocently. The small step seems the most rational one at that given moment, and also proportionate to the desired goal. Who could possibly be opposed to it? New technological delights involving implanted chips are on the increase; it might even be possible to stop behavior by monitoring thought processes (far more effective than leg irons). Besides increasing angst, there are other negative aspects in terms of equality and protection of rights, trust, freedom, and vitality.[20]

"Stop securitization" is the slogan of many civil rights activists, politicians, and intellectuals. Various researchers have spoken out against the cramped nature of the risk society. Bernstein (1998) celebrates living with risk, and De Lint and Kirta (2004) argue in favor of accepting the ambiguity that is part of current society. Yet this hope seems somewhat in vain. Zedner (2009, Chapter 7) argues for that reason (and others) in favor of an overarching "authority for security" that would promote public debate, ethical monitoring, and responsibility and liability in its implementation. The process of securitization seems to be unstoppable, but it can be contained.

A fearful society?!

In this chapter I have sketched a series of shifts of meaning in the arena of criminal law, criminality, safety, precaution, and securitization. This description is obviously open to discussion, especially with regard to empirical research. It is a conceptual history that unfolds against the backdrop of the problem of complexity without direction, as discussed in Part One. Along with the civilizing "defensive" (Chapter 3), I regard the security offensive as a second attempt to create order in this complexity. These two notions have become entangled in the Dutch context. Security gives normative direction via criminal law and reduces complexity. This is difficult to avoid and can have an additional effect – fear.

Sociologists and criminologists tend to regard today's society as "fear-driven" (e.g., Furedi, 1997; Duyvendak et al., 2008). Often politics is credited with sowing fear among the citizenry, or being used to affirm the State's power and to further the interests of the elite. We have encountered this approach in various forms: "governing through crime, risk, punishment, uncertainty, antisocial behaviour" and "through security" (Simon, 2007; O'Malley, 2004; Wacquant, 2009; Ericson, 2007; Crawford, 2009a, 2009b; Zedner, 2009). Crisis situations, it is also argued, are manipulated or even created to push through decisions

(Wolf, 2007). The general sociological consensus is that this is an undesirable development.

In this section I examine the political meaning of the security offensive more precisely. I concur with many traditional scholars that the law has an instrumental function. From Plato to Aquinas there has been discussion of an ordering principle that unfolded under divine law. When church and state were separated during the Age of Reason, the power to create order by law passed explicitly to the state (Hobbes, Kant, Bentham). In modern law schools the function of law has been further fashioned into an instrument for social ordering (Letwin's trichotomy, as reviewed by Witteveen, 2008; see also Ericson, 2007, pp. 16ff.).

This development goes even further. Public morality increasingly coincides with (criminal) law and its compliance and enforcement. This, combined with burgeoning technological possibilities, can take on totalitarian aspects. Let me make a secondary observation about this. Citizens' understanding of "privacy" has changed dramatically. Many control measures are not experienced as undermining privacy, but rather as offering reassurance. In the era of reality shows and the internet, revealing one's "second life" (see Chapter 2) no longer carries the shame it would have in the 1970s, when newly won freedoms made privacy a highly sensitive issue. Technological transparency has normalized these freedoms.

The social unease that feeds securitization derives more from a sense of being unprotected than from being overly controlled.[22] For many decades, World War II was a reference point for moral deliberation. September 11 shifted the mental focus to terrorism. This meant a move from guilt to fear, from the past to the future, from being suspicious of the state to distrusting other citizens (Beck, 2002). Under these conditions, a control state could develop without too much protest, except for a few grumbling jurists and activists. In the case of security, one might even use Adam Smith's famous words, "invisible hand."

It is striking that many security measures are put in place for concrete reasons, the social unrest surrounding these reasons, and a perceived need that something must be done. Usually there is a direct sense of urgency – a party that got out of hand, a returning child molester, a foiled attack. People feel that such things must be prevented, no matter what the price. That does give direction, but the complexity remains. Clearly this also applies to security practices.

The first intervention teams in Rotterdam, which visit "multi-problem families" at home, were made up of representatives from a dozen agencies. They discovered it was only possible to work together within the context presented by specific problem cases. "Yeah, we really are here for everything . . ." (Ombudsman van Rotterdam, 2007).

In practice, securitization requires professionals to work together in complicated relationships.[22] I am even tempted to say that security organizes itself, not because there are political interests with totalitarian needs behind it, but rather because it propagates itself naturally throughout society. Social securitization takes place without totalitarian intentions, which makes its development appear innocent, but it is also more treacherous. Security gives direction in a normative sense by preventing crime, antisocial behavior, and serious threats, but it has developed into a large-scale offensive for social order. Correcting it demands more intelligence than simply being against it.

Of the three programs for ordering, security is the largest and the most successful. In the Netherlands (and also in England) there is a confluence between security and the civilizing program. As an institution, criminal law has played a prominent role in the direction taken by the ordering program. A policy of preventive discipline, drawn from the core function of criminal law enforcement, occupies the moral space. Alarming announcements of potential totalitarianism, however, are in my view of limited applicability. The problems are far too real and the complexity too immense. The question of security in a world without boundaries is a legitimate one, but the situation is too complex to become totalitarian.

Other forms of order are sought as well. The third program I deal with is the attempt to encourage citizen participation. The government hopes that the supposed gap between itself and its citizens can be bridged by involving them. Shared and active citizenship was the great endeavor in the last decade. Its motivation was both social and economic – the labor market, volunteer work, caregiving, and involvement in policy-making. Problems surrounding integration of minorities also played a role. Relations with the citizen even became a theme in the world of security and law. But what, in fact, should be expected of the citizen?

CHAPTER 5

PARTICIPATION AS PANACEA

"The Citizen" is very much the focal point of current interest. He or she is described in many ways, but at the very least this person must be active. "Active citizenship" is now in vogue. The Citizen is no longer a subject (as in the 1950s) or an individual (the 1970s) or a consumer (the 1990s). No, the ideal citizen is a participant, and is preferably self-reliant. This enthusiastic talk about the role of citizens can in fact be interpreted as *commentary*. Society, or in any event the government and often also other citizens, have two complaints about citizens – they are too outspoken and too passive. The lazy consumer, that unwanted creation of the post-war welfare state, is no longer welcome.

The calculating *homo economicus*, who lets nobody stand in his/her way (e.g., Van der Lans, 2005), is out. The Citizen is consumptive[1] and has a short fuse – that's the popular (political) diagnosis. And it must be admitted that The Citizen is also often a pain in the proverbial. Not only fellow citizens but also government officials have much to endure from The Citizen's insolence. For example, police authority has suffered seriously at the hands of The Citizen, or from some citizens, at least. The Citizen appears in current political discourse both as problem and solution. He/she is both a threat to and a guardian angel of the social order. "Live together, work together" was the admonishing motto of the Dutch administration at the end of the last decade.

The active citizen, for example, is explicitly present in the Social Support Act (*Wet maatschappelijke ondersteuning*, Wmo), the legislative framework for healthcare and welfare. The ministry responsible for public health, welfare, and sport propagates this as a "law of participation." Everyone must join in – the young, the handicapped, the homeless, the addicted.

With "social cohesion" as the primary goal, communities, social organizations, and citizens are expected to give shape to "the new welfare" of the Dutch citizen. This Act is unique in that it decentralizes responsibility and moves it to the local level.

I regard this appeal to citizens to be active as a third ordering program – participation – which is in line with civilization and security. The civilizing "defensive" demands preservation, the security offensive promises protection, and the call to the citizenry asks for participation. The call to shared citizenship is also a part of this; it expresses the hope for multi-ethnic convergence. As we have seen, identity and citizenship are closely linked in a globalizing world. Discussions about dual passports, a renewed appreciation of national history, and an insistence on cultural integration are attempts to strengthen and promote national identity. But where does this call for active citizenship come from, and how successful can it be? And, from a democratic perspective, what should we really expect of citizens?

Two forms of citizenship

Until the 1960s, young people in Haarlem who reached the voting age of 23 were given a pamphlet, *Citizenship and civic responsibility*. It contained a frontispiece of Queen Juliana and a foreword from the mayor, and the text began by discussing the "strong will to freedom" of the Dutch people. The text then proceeded to specify that this "will" also has boundaries, and "ends when it comes into conflict with the rules that apply to an orderly society." A little further on, the text is italicized: "Democracy is not just a form of government, it is a civic responsibility (. . .) which lends itself to being laid down in regulations." There is an obvious truth in this statement that cannot be denied. In the decades since the 1960s, however, the word "citizenship" has been meticulously avoided, because it no longer fits with individual emancipation.

Citizenship, however, has made a comeback. In the first decade of the twenty-first century it became a favorite word for politicians and commentators. Citizenship is a complex concept, and its meaning varies according to the historical context. In the fifth century BC Aristotle was the first to elaborate it; he regarded the political freedom of citizens as the essence of being human (Faulks, 2000, p. 14). This laid the foundation for classical republicanism, in which Faulks distinguishes three aspects. The *scope* determines who is and is not allowed citizenship. The *content* tells us which laws and responsibilities are involved in it. The *thickness* expresses the activities expected of citizens. Ideas about these aspects can and do shift.

In the seventeenth and eighteenth centuries, citizenship was primarily a cultural status (Dekker & De Hart, 2005). It depended, for example, on being a member of a guild and taking part in the local militia. This "civil" sense echoed the idea of civic virtues; these were later ridiculed as bourgeois, but have been rediscovered in the last few years. The idea of state citizenship – a body of rights derived from membership in the constitutional state – developed around 1800, when nation-states began to emerge. It concerned who did (and who did not) fall under state authority and could claim protection as such. Citizenship has both a constitutional and a civil aspect; it is about the relation between citizens and the state, and between citizens and the community.

This distinction is of great importance in the current discussion about active citizenship, which deals specifically with civil citizenship. Democratic citizenship is also being discussed currently (Stewart, 1995; in the Netherlands, De Winter, 2005). Because of the linguistic affinity with civil society, I prefer the term civil citizenship. In 1963 Marshall was one of the first to emphasize these communitarian aspects of citizenship: "based on loyalty to a civilization which is a common possession" (cited in Stewart, 1995, p. 68). Instead of embarking on a more detailed discussion of the political nature of citizenship,[2] let me simply state the following. State citizenship is regulated by the legal rights and responsibilities of citizens, and civil citizenship is about the citizens' "willingness" to contribute actively to the quality of society.

In the 1960s, apparently, it was thought (cf. the pamphlet in Haarlem) that constitutional citizenship (the right to vote) should be reflected in the importance of being civic-minded. The emerging individualization owes something to that. Previously, the government could leave the development of civil citizenship to the disciplining functions of priests, pastors, and political leaders. Once these pillars of society had disappeared, citizenship found itself in a totally different context. Civil citizenship was set free, so to speak (and that pamphlet on civic responsibility disappeared in the cupboard). The results of this, and their interpretation, have more than filled the previous chapters.

Just when those pillars of Dutch society were vanishing, large groups of foreigners started to stream into the country – initially by invitation. These foreigners had not been initiated into the "secret language" of norms in the individualized society. Some of the second-generation immigrants have difficulty finding their way through the relatively labyrinthine institutions of the Dutch welfare state. And many of the natives feel an increasing rage at the loss of their familiar surroundings (De Gruijter et al., 2010). "Citizens are still citizens, but they are uncertain of which city and of whose city," Castells remarked somewhat casually (2004, p. 414). State citizenship is no longer self-evident,[3] and civil citizenship needs to be reinvented. This is the context in which the call for active citizenship is made.

People wanted

The search for active citizenship begins with the supposition that there is a gap between government institutions and citizens. This gap is not easy to explain; it has to do with issues discussed earlier such as individualization, globalization, and the advance of technology. It also has to do equally with commercialization of the media, the development of social welfare, and the changing population demographics. In other words, the gap has many causes. For this reason, it makes sense to approach "the gap" from a more pragmatic perspective: How well do citizens and institutions interface, really? The Janus-like figure of The Citizen as both problem and solution raises the question of whether they really go together. Essentially, the question is about the legitimacy of democracy and the relations between citizens and institutions that must support and buttress this democracy.

A political-party system assumes, for example, that citizens inform themselves and are on occasion prepared to vote. It also assumes a certain degree of active participation in politics. Above all, the majority of citizens must allow themselves to be represented. As Van Gunsteren put it, citizenship is more than a status – it is postulated on autonomy and the ability to exercise good judgment, so that the citizen is capable of "both ruling and being ruled" (1988, p. 732). Few would dare argue that the political system has no problem in this regard. De Beus (2003) speaks of a democracy of spectators. Politics is desperately seeking the citizen, which fits in with its role in a democratic society, and sometimes that takes on populist forms.

Other institutions seem to show a "gap" as well. There is a decline in the once-normal confidence that citizens placed in the police, the legal system, education, and healthcare – it is not dramatic, but enough to be problematic. More specifically, trust in a number of political democratic institutions went into a free-fall in 2001-2004, after which it recovered somewhat. In general, appreciation for the democratic system in the Netherlands is high compared with other European nations (taken from Verhoeven, 2009, pp. 27ff.). Despite this, citizens and institutions seem to be estranged from each other. Pim Fortuyn, the Dutch populist politician, spoke of an "orphaned society" (2002).

Citizens are demanding and professionals are often uncertain (Tonkens, 2008). It seems as though the relation between professionals or officials and the citizen has become somewhat "unbuffered." An obvious and shared frame of reference – a cohesive totality of protocols, ideas, and behaviors that are essentially undisputed – seems to be missing. We know, for example, what to expect from the doctor and the teacher, and they in turn know more or less what is expected of them. Without this kind of implicit agreement, the citizen does not know what (s)he should be doing (and hence regularly crosses the line), the professional is uncertain of his/her status (and hence views the client as a threat), and the government lacks a legitimate steering mechanism (and hence improvises freely).

"The gap" refers especially to *a lack of a common narrative*, in which officials, professionals, and citizens can interact with each other. This creates a situation in which the welfare society is desperately seeking its citizens. It doesn't take much to show that The Citizen does not exist; as a result, various typologies of citizens have been proposed in recent decades. Van den Brink (2002, pp. 76-86) lists the hard-working, the uncomplaining, and the endangered citizen; Spangenburg et al. (2001) name the inactive, the dependent, the pragmatic, and the responsible citizen; Becker and Dekker (2005) refer to the indifferent, the dissatisfied, the trustworthy, and the involved citizen; and Verhoeven (2004) writes of the active, dependent, expectant, and impartial citizen. That is quite a variety of types for the government to find. All sorts of people are wanted.

This is not only a governmental need however. Political representation is becoming more difficult to achieve, and so the need for direct influence also arises among citizens. Fung and Wright (2001) write about "empowered deliberative democracy," an actively negotiating democracy with certain characteristics. This democracy deals with specific problems and addresses them with a practical approach from the bottom up, in which active citizens confer formally with professionals and authority figures. Bang and Sørenson (1999) called such new active citizens "everyday makers." New institutions may even emerge from this approach. A Dutch example is neighborhood mediation, or voluntary conflict resolution in residential areas. This new organization arose at the local level (Peper, 1998); it maintains relations with the municipality and the police, and offers practical solutions (described in Fiers & Jansen, 2004).

Tonkens et al. (2006a) have researched other initiatives similar to this that sprang up outside the purview of government and professionals. The precipitating factor is usually an acute problem. Often their success depends on the closeness of their contacts, both internal and external. They are divided into four categories based on the number of contacts. Successful initiatives often develop from "light" projects (few contacts) to "federative projects" (many contacts). Participants in the projects expect to be taken seriously and to be accepted by the government as partners in dialogue. That is by no means always the case.

The authors point out that there is not much "connection" among population groups, unless that is an explicit goal. Active citizens are predominantly white, well educated, and older, given the required skills. Less educated citizens are interested, but lack sufficient self-confidence (Tonkens et al., 2006a, p. 59). In other words, citizens are not only sought, but also offer their services, albeit selectively. In this way "a market for citizenship" develops. Verhoeven (2009) notes in his epilogue, however, that ultimately the government is not open to criticism and does not respond well to the emotions aroused. Yet sometimes citizens are found – usually the hard-working, involved, responsible, and active ones.

Citizens in security

Citizen participation in the security arena is an interesting example of the meaning of active citizenship, given the security offensive described earlier. The dual approach to the citizen as both problem and solution is most evident here. Whether as a consumer of security, a suspect, or a disrespectful oaf (Van Stokkom, 2010), the citizen is a problem. Yet the citizen becomes the solution in a variety of ways, by becoming involved in policy-making and in practice (see Terpstra & Kouwenhoven, 2004; Terpstra, 2008; Scholte, 2008; Van Caem, 2008). Citizen participation then goes far beyond giving statements or testifying (the traditional civilian roles in aiding the police), and involves more than simply adding extra locks and alarms to one's residence and vehicles (which Van Dijk, 2008b, regards as the most important reason for the decline in crime).

Security problems as such are well suited to citizen participation because of the perceived urgency (e.g., nuisance), but also because of the communal frame of reference. In general, the norm is shared and the goal is clear. Citizens are then quite active in security. Scholte (2008) categorized different kinds of citizen participation over a two-year period based on newspaper reports.[4] He listed *surveillance*, both passive and active (e.g., SMS Alert or emergency text messaging), *relational control* (e.g., neighborhood volunteers), and *conflict resolution* (such as the neighborhood resolution role mentioned above).

Other forms of participation are policy-making[5] and policy recommendations (which can take various forms). Finally, there are residents who organize their own security. This is normal in malls and shopping centers, but also in gated communities.[6] "Actual break-ins and vandalism seem to mobilize citizens" (Scholte, 2008, p. 229). Scholte also notes, in agreement with Terpstra and Kouwenhoven (2004), that there is little representation in this area, although he does point out initiatives from under-represented groups (youths and immigrants).

The "citizen in security" thus provides service in many forms, from "eyes and ears" or as an extension of the police, to adviser and policy consultant. Using Scholte's classification, Van Caem (2008, p. 15) listed 457 projects in Amsterdam, each of which involved an average of ten residents (for a total of approximately 5,000). Most took part in a tour of the neighborhood, looking as a group for problem areas in need of attention. In all cases there was a relationship between the residents and the police and/or the municipality. Van Caem noted two problems with the collaboration – a professional barrier and an administrative ceiling. At the end of the day, either the professionals laid claim to the problem, or the residents ran into reluctance or lack of comprehension from the administration, usually at district level (see also Van Caem et al., 2010).

This raises the question of the (supposed) interest in citizen participation. In general, it is assumed that active citizens contribute to the social quality of their environment, which keeps security problems in check. There is talk of "collective efficacy," a term that takes on an interesting meaning in Carr (2005; see also Terpstra, 2008, p. 246). Carr distinguishes different forms of control – in the private sphere (family and friends), in the public sphere (municipal services and police), and also in what he calls the "parochial" sphere (clubs, volunteer organizations, schools, and churches). Carr describes this new form of parochialism as "a set of practices that creates solutions at the parochial level but owes its existence and its efficacy to the intervention of institutions and groups from outside the neighborhood" (cited by Terpstra, 2008, p. 248). This is about relations between organizations (government and non-government) and citizens, which generate a new kind of collective power. Terpstra (2008) thinks that similar networks in the Netherlands are not nearly as effective. There is too much institutional thinking, and citizens are often regarded as troublesome (as noted above.) Terpstra even speaks of an "institutional imperialism" (p. 264), in which citizens are squeezed into an institutional corset.

Van Stokkom (2008, 2010) also criticizes the "rhetoric of self-reliance" in security policy, which he regards as more sociological hope than reality. Citizens usually remain aloof and feel powerless in actual security situations, yet he also points out that participation increases citizens' trust in the police, other professionals, and local security policies (p. 275). A small number of people do want to contribute; "the trick is to identify them" (p. 278). There is a great deal of tension between assigning responsibility and accepting it. The connection between a pro-active government and participating citizens is apparently fragile. Perhaps their mutual expectations do not coincide.

Counter democracy

The "active citizenship" ordering program is looking for a communal narrative; after much trial and error, it is developing. What it all comes down to is a selective interest among citizens (in terms of participation and topics), a large chance of failure without professional support, simultaneous resistance from professionals, and a reluctant government. The emotional responses of people can be shocking, and the critical input hard for the administration to swallow (Verhoeven, 2009). To borrow Van Stokkom's terminology, this is more vain hope than actual progress. Let's also look at these results from two different perspectives. First, some solid results have been achieved with citizen participation. Above I cited the example of neighborhood resolution, but there are many other examples of successful volunteer work and social commitment (for example, in patient organizations and in sports; Overbeek et al., 2008).

There are also theoretical reasons for looking at the criticism of citizen participation from another standpoint. Consider the importance of counter democracy, in which the role of citizens should be viewed not simply in terms of participation, but also as a counterweight, or as organized skepticism. Rosanvallon and Goldhammer (2008) point out that there is always a certain tension between the legitimacy of democratic institutions and the degree of trust placed in them. To put it bluntly, you don't have to trust them as such in order to accept them (and vice versa). A democracy can strengthen, suppress, or even make explicit the tension between the two.

Historically, three forms have developed for explication – vigilance, civil disobedience, and civil rights (Rosanvallon & Goldhammer, 2008). The first took the form of public opinion, which the media make visible. In recent years the media have proliferated enormously. Civil disobedience can take a variety of forms – from refusing to pay taxes to squatters' riots and eco-terrorism. The third form, civil rights, comes from judicial verdicts, but can also take other forms in which citizens arbitrate. In fact, parliamentary democracy, according to Van Gunsteren (2006), is a form of organized skepticism. The current era has produced forms that the authors quoted have described as unpolitical counter democracy.

Counter democracy can take the form of positive activism, but also of disillusioned nihilism. The latter is growing strongly against the backdrop of the government's changed situation. Rosanvallon and Goldhammer regard current populism as an acute manifestation of the present political clutter and argue for a "modern mixed regime" (2008, p. 290f.). In the first place, it involves a policy of deliberative democracy, aimed at maximizing citizen participation in decision-making. In the second place, a better organization of the counter democratic process, in the form of "citizen evaluation boards" and "citizen watch dog groups" (the neighborhood trouble-shooting tours in Amsterdam are an example of this). Finally, the authors (p. 306) argue for "restoring a vision of a common world."

The problem of the unpolitical counter democracy is never a lack of will, but of significance. Significance must be visible in the democracy's achievements – an orderly world based on clear interpretations, a symbolization of collective power that people want to belong to and believe in, and ways for dealing with disagreement and conflict. When placed in the broader context of the importance of counter democracy, citizen participation takes on a different perspective. The idea of maximum participation and integration no longer dominates. Instead the idea of a constructive counterweight prevails, along with acknowledgment of the rough spots and fuss that accompany it.

Politicians and policy-makers tend to regard participation, social networks, and social capital as a great common good – "an urban policy fix . . . a magic bullet" (Blokland & Savage, 2008, p. 3). The community, however, has always been a place of both cohesion and protest, of coming together and of struggle. These authors resist the romantic idea of a network urban environment, in which social capital and creativity blossom, and existing power differences and inequalities can be forgotten. Ultimately it is about the resources and the possibilities for developing social capital in a network of relationships – and the struggle for them.

The ordering program aimed at active citizenship runs into problems because of selective citizen participation and unrealistic expectations. This comes down to a matter of reluctant professionals and unwilling administrators. Participation also means facing differences in power, contradictions, and conflicts between citizens and with citizens. Citizen participation is important because representative democracy has lost its significance, yet at the same time it is difficult to get it off the ground. The perspective of counter democracy is more appropriate here. A communal narrative can only develop when there are well-defined positions and mutual respect. What should the government, institutions, and citizens ultimately expect from each other?

Moral challenge

To better clarify the moral appeal for active citizens, it makes sense to distinguish between norms that reject negative behavior and those that prescribe positive behavior. In the first instance, one can rely on a basic libertarian concept, the harm principle. This principle goes back to John Stuart Mill (1859), who used it to legitimize intervention by the state. If one citizen causes harm to another, then the state may intervene; "your freedom does not extend to the point that I suffer under it." In the second instance one starts from a positive idea about the good life and society. It can be interpreted to mean that the government may also prescribe what is good for the people (see also Chapter 3).

We also find this difference in Isaiah Berlin's (1969) famous distinction between negative and positive freedom. Negative freedom refers to the domain in which a person can, undisturbed by others, do or be whatever is within his/her power. Positive freedom refers to the value of community, cultural identity, and cultural self-determination. Government ideas about the second value can undermine the first form of freedom. But a nakedly libertarian negative freedom contributes little to communality. In our culture and era, the good life is first and foremost an individual matter. Under libertarian conditions, there is no legitimacy for a government opinion about the good life.

In recent decades the harm principle has become reality. "Victimhood" has grown into a category that directs everyday moral practice. Both government and civil society have become quite reticent about what is considered good. Instead we let ourselves be led by that which we reject: humiliation, cruelty, and discrimination determine moral choices in an era without illusions (Boutellier, 1993). It seems to me there are good reasons why "victim morality" ultimately fails in a complex world without direction – morality being the daily consensus on public norms and values. It is too flimsy, too narrow, and too relative.

It is too *flimsy* in the sense that it is ultimately not capable of regulating relationships between citizens. Dalrymple (see Chapter 3) and Field (see Chapter 4) are right in that a certain "buffer of civilization" is necessary for a reassuring predictability in the behavior of others. The increase in crime, nuisance behavior, antisocial behavior, and indecent behavior in recent decades – which can be summed up as general incivility (Van Stokkom, 2010) – points to a lack of empathic ability, that psychological category *par excellence* for "victimalized morality" (Boutellier, 1993). Challenging this particular virtue of empathy sometimes seems to be an inherent part of youth culture nowadays (Chapter 2). Empathy clearly needs to be more widely inculcated if it is not to be the subject of provocation. Empathy requires training based on higher ideals.

In a world without boundaries, a victimalized morality is also too *narrow* for an orderly society. It belongs to an individualized society, and offers too little community experience. A world without boundaries however has a different sort of communality from that of the past. Solidarity is not imposed from the outside; instead there is an inner willingness to take a positive attitude toward others. We can imagine ourselves in the position of the other, and we hope that the other can do the same for us. According to Komter (2005), this reciprocity – interpreted as reciprocal exchange of everything that can be exchanged (information, services, gifts, support) – lays the foundation for every form of common ground and is fully applicable to relations in a world without boundaries. It is based on recognition of the other and the willingness to give and to give back – even at a later time – and in that sense extends further than a victimalized morality.

Finally, there is a third reason: a victimalized morality is too relative. Dutch society, with its flimsy and narrow-minded morality, is confronted with newcomers who have more robust normative positions to uphold. Many Muslim communities share an absolute religious belief, yet such absolute beliefs were rejected in the Netherlands after World War II. The libertarian mentality seems somewhat meager in comparison to the robust politico-religious ideology which is Islam for many Muslims. Islam makes Dutch society painfully aware that Western achievements, such as non-discrimination against women and homosexuals, have more fundamental roots than the rejection of victimhood. That argument suffices within a libertarian context, but fails when it comes to absolutist religious beliefs. Reciprocity is important here as well (Komter, 2005).[7]

The call for active citizenry fails if there is no agreement about what the appeal should consist of. Let me clarify this. Empathy is based on being able to imagine the situation of the other, and reciprocity asks for recognition of the other. Both must be taught and practiced in order to be effective. This is what gives legitimacy to the ordering program for citizenship. Let me take that a step further. Ideas about "the good life" (that classic philosophical question) are privatized in a libertarian context. We may decide what we find positive, but to be able to do that, we have to develop ourselves.

To learn what we regard as good, we have to be educated, and not just by having ideals given to us, but by having options. Ideals mean challenge. In that sense conservative traditions can be relevant – not as a natural good, but as a set of interesting ideas. Being able to choose freely for "a specific good life" also means deliberation and rejection of other options. A victimalized morality is not motivated to reflect on what is good. The good needs to be challenged, without being prescribed. It may lack the moral coherence of the past, but that is no reason not to experience it.

Taken together, "deterioration" of social etiquette, lack of challenge from positive ideals, and weakness of cultural relativism are reasons to rethink our moral principles. I would like to reformulate the appeal to citizens in this context. Hope can be found in the communal narrative of citizens and institutions, namely, the hope of redesigning moral space, not as a given but as a process. And therein lies the importance of civilization – the acknowledgment of identity poses the question of considerations about good and evil, ideas about a good life, and opinions about one's relationships to others. If one notices that lack of civilization also consists of "not being heard," then one should definitely speak out. Not in a noncommittal way, but in a forceful and challenging manner. Hope in institutions is useless if at least some citizens are not willing to contribute. It is legitimate to challenge citizens to do this. This is how social continuity develops.

Multi-ethnic continuity

Active citizenship contains the hope for shared citizenship; Schinkel (2008) sees this more as a demand than a hope. Problems surrounding integration are also a focal point in the call for citizen participation. Van Dale, the definitive dictionary of the Dutch language, defines integration as "being included in a whole," but this is too general to describe the reciprocal demands and expectations between the dominant culture and the minority group. Relations between the "new Dutch"[8] and Dutch society are too diverse. Most Chinese speak hardly any Dutch, but go about quietly in the anonymity of large cities. Moroccan hooligans often speak perfect Dutch (with a local accent), but still cause society much trouble. Violent Antillean youths rarely know any Dutch, yet they have Dutch passports. In a society as complex and lacking direction as the Netherlands, it is unclear how and where one is supposed to integrate.[9]

For this reason, it is sensible to discriminate between various forms of being "included," based on the need for social continuity. Approximately 50,000 youths leave school without a diploma each year (WRR, 2009), which forms a calculable risk for the Dutch economy. Calls for violence and discrimination against women, homosexuals, and "the decadent West" are in direct conflict with the acquired values of a pluralistic Western culture. Loitering youth who routinely intimidate residents are an unacceptable violation of the public nature of open spaces. These are signs that continuity is being threatened. For this reason I regard assimilation, participation, and preservation of identity as legitimate principles for the inclusion of minority groups, *depending on the topic under discussion*.

Assimilation can be expected with regard to the legal system and the libertarian pluralism that it protects. The pluralistic nature of Dutch society implies recognition of the right to develop one's own identity, on the condition that it does not harm others. Culturally, this means freedom of expression, a willingness to engage in self-reflection, and the ability to feel what others feel (empathy). Residents of this nation endorse these principles, at least through behavior, and uphold the principles of the rule of law. The legal system and the rule of law are *virtually* nonnegotiable principles of society.[10] I temper this statement with "virtually," because this is not the end of history – there is always the potential for change.

Participation can be expected in the areas of education, work, and income. Dutch society benefits when there is maximum participation in the work force. If too large a segment of the population is not able to contribute constructively to its own support, this threatens the general level of prosperity. From a cultural perspective, this means that one speaks Dutch and does not withdraw from the prevailing forms of social intercourse (for example, by wearing face veils). This principle is double-edged. The country of destination (Scheffer, 2007) commits itself to creating conditions for participation, and the immigrants to demonstrating their willingness to participate.

Finally, there is the right to culture and *identity*. The current cultural climate seems to dismiss the psychological importance of "one's own" too easily. Walzer (2004) shows that we assume, falsely, that relationships in a modern society are "voluntary," and we can simply exit them. We are dealing with "passionate identities" that also play a role in the political and social arenas. It is important to acknowledge them, but without tolerating their dangerous forms. A pluralistic society supports the legitimacy of different traditions, customs, and various etiquettes. These should be respected insofar as they are not in conflict with the demands of legal assimilation and socioeconomic participation. In principle, identity is free.

With this somewhat normative conclusion to this section, I have tried to formulate the citizen's perspective in such a way that it can be a starting point for Part Three. In a globalizing, network society, a democratic mindset is not an obvious and self-evident product of society. It leads to an appeal for active and participating citizenship, but this appeal is not without problems. It develops through a process of trial and error amid overly high expectations. The idea of counter democracy gives a more realistic picture of the importance of and possibilities for citizen participation. It compels the government to take a more explicit position.

In a normative sense, government and society have found themselves in a negative consensus. Victimhood – rejection of cruelty, humiliation, and discrimination – is the definitive moral argument in a non-ideological world. Yet "victimalized morality" is too flimsy, too narrow, and too relative to guarantee social continuity in a world without boundaries. This leads to a constitutional dilemma. Social continuity in the community implies that the government plays a role in its ordering, yet taking an explicit moral position means conflict with its own constitutional principles. The government can make demands in terms of the rule of law and the legal system (hence the security offensive), and socioeconomic participation (not dealt with in this book). But, in principle, identity is free.

It is in this context that I argue for a normative policy, within institutions, of empathy, reciprocity, and challenge. Empathy entails the basic competence to relate to one's immediate environment. Reciprocity means acknowledging the other and a willingness to give and to give back. And challenge is "the ideal of stimulating ideals." The network society has no plausible great narratives to achieve social ordering, nor can such ordering be imposed from above. We can, however, appeal to one another for ideas about what the good life is. This hints at a public morale of challenge and confrontation, but without expecting to have the last word.

PART III THE ORDER OF IMPROVISATION

The programs of recent decades has taught us a great deal about the desires, motives, and approaches involved in organizing a world without boundaries. What presents itself as complexity without direction is regulated and restrained by approaches from civilization, security, and citizenship. These programs indicate the importance of moral direction in human complexity. In Part Three, I develop a new perspective on the central theme of this book: the design and arrangement of moral space – its organization, content, and process.

Thanks to myriad connections – both physical and digital – the world has shrunk. Once-distant corners are now much closer, which has immeasurably expanded the environments in which people live and work. This historically unprecedented access has made life more chaotic, even if only in our perception of it. I look for the principles of social ordering behind the ongoing tension between complexity (without direction) and the attempts to organize it. Which mechanisms are involved and how can institutions define them?

To begin I discuss the conditions of the "nodal universe." According to the sociologist Manuel Castells, we are dealing with a new form of society that is based on the network character of the current information age. The second half of Chapter 6 looks at complexity theories in the scientific world, and Chapters 7 and 8 address social complexity. Much attention is devoted to the function of authority, which is crucial to normative direction in law, formal and informal regulation, and everyday life.

The determining mechanism in human networks is ultimately fine-tuning. It is the search by one identity for harmony with another, and vice versa, that creates social order. For that reason, I speak of the improvising society – the totality of fine-tuning processes in the environment. To that end I return to complexity theories in the final chapter. This tuning is shaped by incidents, initiatives, and the centers of gravity created by powerful institutions whose core functions define their spheres of influence. Through it all, the improvising society seeks the middle way, between hopeless cacophony and scintillating polyphony.

CHAPTER 6

THE NODAL UNIVERSE

The first five chapters focused on describing and analyzing the manifestations of what I call the world without boundaries. They dealt with the contradictions, discontent and rage, and the attempts to find direction. This chapter is primarily about complexity. I examine the formal conditions for complexity in current society; the resulting insights will allow us to discuss what I call the improvising society. The question of ordering arises when there is a new arrangement of social forms, or "social morphology" (after Castells, 2000a, p. 500). There are new global relations, new forms of production and consumption, and new social conditions, all of which are based on a new resource – information.

All these innovations, sociologically speaking, fall within the concept of the network society. Nodes and links are seemingly intangible components of current society. The observation that we live in a network society is not particularly new; it could even be viewed as somewhat old-fashioned.[1] "Network" (the noun) has become a basic concept in the natural and social sciences, economics, and politics. It is also playing an increasingly larger role in everyday life. "Networking" (the verb) has morphed into a social skill.

No matter how fashionable "networking" might seem, it points to a social reality that reaches far beyond cocktail parties and golf courses. Every internet user understands intuitively what it means. Social organizations understand the need to expand their "links" to other "nodes." Social ordering – the design of moral space through organization, content, and process – has now entered the era of the nodal universe.[2] Unlike the rest of the book, this chapter is somewhat abstract, because it searches for the morphology of complexity.

Complexity contains more order than we are inclined to think, but it requires a different sort of vocabulary. To that end I call on network science and chaos theory, along with the science of complex systems. This can be somewhat precarious because their terminology comes from a different library, one primarily devoted to the "hard" sciences. Despite this, I have conscientiously hacked my way through in order to verbalize the relation between complexity and social order. First I look at the information era and its networking mindset, after which I examine three tenets from the study of complex systems.

The information era

For an enlightening description of the "world without boundaries" I begin with the work of the Catalan sociologist Manuel Castells. In the 1990s he wrote three massive volumes on *The information age* (revised editions 2000a, 2004, 2000b), which are a major landmark in sociology. He analyzed changes in the economy, politics, and culture, and relations between states, organizations, and citizens. He places them convincingly within the Information Technology Paradigm (ITP). Castells was the author who analyzed in detail the comprehensive term "information age." His analysis is most relevant; let me summarize it.

A different space

Information technology facilitates a process of increasing globalization and individualization; the import of this process cannot be overestimated.[3] The information era opens a new space; Castells calls this the "space of flows." This space arises between nodal points that are connected to each other. This "space of flows" differs from the "space of places," which is constructed and experienced physically. Societies are increasingly organizing themselves in the flows between the nodes – flows of capital, information, technology, interaction among organizations, of images, sounds, and symbols, and of people (Castells, 2000a, p. 442).

The new modes of being that arise from this have major consequences for social bonds. In fact, they form a threat to traditional communities, cultures, neighborhoods, and families:[4] the "space of places" that offer people peace, security, and shelter. Physical institutions have not disappeared, but are now part of a new world of media and internet usage, mobility, and flexibility.[5] Identity formation based on functions and community has been replaced with more fluid forms of identity production. Networks organize around the individual body. Consider, for example, the culture of the designer body (Koops et al., 2009) and the dominant role of sports – and their total opposite, the body-concealing *burqa* and *niqab*.

The dismantling of old social structures does not happen without a struggle – the network society creates discontent and resistance. In *The power of identity* Castells (2004) describes the counter movements called forth by the network society. Many have organized themselves around "primary identities," such as religion, ethnicity, and nationality. This explains the fundamentalism among Christians in the United States, and among Muslims both in the West and in the Muslim world. There are also new collective identities, such as the environmental movement.[6] "Our societies are constituted by the interaction between the 'net' and 'the self,' between the network society and the power of identity" (Castells, 2000b, p. 383).

The most dramatic development, according to Castells (2004, p. 133f.), is that which takes place around the nation state. Networks create power bases outside the state – international networks of capital, production, communication, organized crime, multinational institutions, supranational military powers, non-governmental organizations (NGOs), transnational religions, international opinion groups, terrorist groups, and other social movements. At the national level we see a similar shift to local powers, introverted communities, new tribal bonds, cults, and gangs. The state is "too small to handle global forces, yet too big to manage people's lives" (Castells, 2004, p. 337).[7]

No matter how, the modern state must relate to the complexity of global and local networks. A network state, which can only survive when connected to other nodes, is emerging (Castells, 2004, p. 130). This impacts and changes the state's legitimacy for intervention – from representation of the will of the people to the capacity to bring forth order out of complexity. In the previous section I described three programs for this, but the government is only partially successful in these endeavors, which undermines its political credibility. This can be seen daily in the media. The electorate is becoming increasingly unpredictable, there is more room for single-issue parties, and there is increasing scrutiny of politicians' integrity.[8]

This does not mean that government has become irrelevant; perhaps the opposite is the case. Although the state has lost its central position, it remains one of the last beacons in the storm of globalization. This fundamental contradiction defines the current state of politics – it must navigate between being impotent and enforcing, between giving space and creating order. Saskia Sassen,[9] the globalization specialist, regards the state not as a victim of, but rather as a prerequisite for, globalization. Territory, legislation, economy, security, authority, and membership are all national constructs on which the process of globalization takes place.

Sassen (2006, p. 343) thinks that Castells' macro-perspective has caused him to overlook the fact that globalization is a form of "denationalization." It can be highly selective – it might, for example, only affect the financial sector – while there is also a policy of renationalization as related to the immigration issue. The national level has not been eliminated, but rather has acquired a different meaning. Sassen's (p. 379f.) detailed analysis shows that the digital era offers the potential to act both globally and locally. The nation-state continues to perform a key role, but, simultaneously, that role is changing profoundly.

Other authors also emphasize the continuing importance of the state. It represents symbolic power and cultural authority. The state has the law as the source of its legitimacy; the government can coordinate and inform. If it comes to it, the state also has the power of the sword – the monopoly of violence in the police, judicial system, and the military (as argued by Crawford, 2006;

Loader & Walker, 20006). We could say that, along with Sassen and others, Castells should not exaggerate. Developments flow from the neighborhood to the world and then back again. It is here that we encounter the grotesque word "glocalization" (Robertson, 1992), in which nation-states continue to play an intermediary role.

Living together in networks

In his three-volume work Castells sketches a radically changing world, but also one of local deterioration. He portrays impotent states and alienated citizens. The information era shreds, the network society is disordered, and the ensuing reactions are rigid and intolerant. Globalized individualization leads ultimately to chaos, which only the most cheerful of intellectuals regard as an inviting prospect. One might even ask if the world without boundaries can be understood in anything but negative terms.

A shredded society is not a necessary end result of these developments. Information technology, globalization, and individualization create a different world, but not necessarily a chaotic society. What we have to do is learn how to perceive it and how to understand the new order. Sassen points out that nation-states are not being overwhelmed; rather, they are participating in the globalization. In my opinion, something similar applies to the culture of the network society. Let me explore this further, with the help of Jan van Dijk, the Dutch communications researcher.

In 1991[10] Van Dijk first published a book in Dutch titled *The network society.*[11] He too (1999) criticized the "one-dimensional" character of Castells' analyses, because it suggested that network carriers – individuals, groups, organizations – are nolonger important, almost as if they ceased to exist. An all-engulfing "space of flows" is not a realistic representation, in Van Dijk's opinion. Networks are collections of connections between elements of a certain kind. They occur in a variety of forms – physical, technological, and social – yet they are inconceivable without the basic elements.

The essence of a network is connection; more specifically, connecting creates an opening. Van Dijk regards this as "the secret of networking as an organizing principle" (2006, p. 30). "Opening" offers enormous potential for the organization of independent units. It creates possibilities for units to adapt to their environment, and this – which is important here – leads to the production of order. Van Dijk emphatically chose an approach that begins with elements or units (individuals, households, organizations), which are then connected. The network society is "a social formation with an infrastructure of social and media networks enabling its prime mode of organization at all levels" (Van Dijk, 2006, p. 20).

In today's culture, networks of individuals form the basis for societal organization. This is in contrast to ideological "mass societies," in which the collective organizes the individual. The historical uniqueness of this form of organization can possibly be contested – there have always been networks – but the scale and size of cooperation have grown enormously (2006, pp. 21-23). Mass society was characterized by a high degree of internal connectedness and limited openness to the outside world. The pillarization of Dutch society in the twentieth century is a good example. In contrast, the structure of the network society is less intensely collectivized; it is polycentric, less inclusive.

Van Dijk, however, rejects radical ideas about the network society. It is not the ideal democratic society, but neither is it a world without social cohesion. He gives his view of the network society in a list of ten points (2006, p. 37f.), which I hammer together below. In the network society, relations between units are increasingly important, as are the elements themselves, which remain linked to their physical environment. The number of direct relations increases via both social and media networks. This creates a new social infrastructure, in which the media (including the internet) start to function as an independent entity.

Interactions in the network society are multilateral and intensive (e.g., Web 2.0), with new forms of organization that vary along such dimensions as centralized/decentralized, open/closed, scale magnification/reduction. These organizational forms can no longer be guided bureaucratically; instead, they are "infocratic" (from Zuurmond, 1994). To reduce complexity, networks must be more controlled and coded – the opposite of the much-desired informal decision-making. This leads to increasing selectivity and the exclusion of units from access to networks. Relations in a network society are ultimately relatively uncertain; there is a high probability of "hypes," political earthquakes, and social eruptions.

The network society is a reality. But just as Sassen emphasizes that the nation-state continues to play an important role (albeit a different one), Van Dijk asks us to focus on the continuing relevance of physical nodes, be they individuals, households, or organizations. Let me add to that the overarching level of social institutions – the legal system, education, healthcare, business, and the like. Social order in a world without boundaries is still based on institutions, even though these institutions must function in a totally new context. Van Dijk puts overblown expectations for the network society in perspective, neither does he agree with the image of an all-devouring, all-shredding globalization.

Social consequences

We should not make the world without boundaries seem newer than it is, yet the social consequences of the technologically driven development of the network society are nevertheless enormous. With the help of Van Dijk, let me list a number of them. First, there is an increasing *integration of technology* into a sort of super technology – "a fully integrated and all-embracing infrastructure of the network society" (2006, p. 43). This concerns information technology, communications technology, biotechnology, and nanotechnology. This super technology has advantages, but it also contributes to the growth of the "surveillance society" (Lyon, 2001). Data overkill can be so huge that it may even solve the privacy problem by reducing it to a problem of insignificance.[12] Here is not the place, however, to give this serious consideration (for a nuanced review, see Van 't Hof et al., 2010).

In *economy*, there is a new dimension, a faster one that is independent of time and place. The new economy based on information as resource has also taken off. The shadow aspects of this need no elaboration, but the social aspects are relevant. Classic steering mechanisms (bureaucracy, physical infrastructure, and mass communication) are less applicable. For a very long time office work was slower and more expensive than manufacturing, but the era of Taylorism is long past.[13] The office is now an information system, "generating, producing, collecting, processing, multiplying, distributing, storing, retrieving and interpreting data" (Van Dijk, 2006, p. 69).

Politics and government are also re-forming themselves according to network logic. Van Dijk makes an important point, for my purpose, when he proposes that the network society not only has horizontal but also vertical relations between nodes. The state is among the strongest (combination of) actors (2006, p. 101), yet the state's organization has changed radically. The central characteristics of bureaucracy, such as hierarchy and central organization, are under pressure. In principle, Van Dijk (p. 125) thinks the state can go in one of two directions – toward a stronger state under the aegis of security and effectiveness, or toward a weaker one that allows a great deal of room for the market and civil society.

The relation between the government and the individual citizen deserves special attention. This falls under the heading of privacy, a concept than can be defined in many ways. On the one hand, there is freedom from interference by the state, on the other, the right to a private life (also in regard to fellow citizens). The essence of a network, however, is openness. More opportunities for using and misusing it keep emerging – tracking technology, data mining, profiling, and the like. It would seem that privacy should be one of the great tenets of the network society, yet the opposite is the case.

With respect to *social infrastructure*, it is important to note that information technology leads not only to an expansion of the world (or, as Giddens, 1991, puts it, "time-space distantiation"). There is also contraction, a reduction of the time-space dimensions. This duality is also apparent in the relation between public space and private domain. There is talk of the "privatization" of public spaces, and at the same time of the "colonization"[13] of individual lives (Van Dijk, 2006, p. 161).[14] Intimidating behavior by youths on the street is paired, for example, with teams of professionals coming to inspect what happens behind their closed doors.[16] The cell phone may have given the individual public space, but the internet has pushed right through to the bedroom.

Although "blurring spheres of living" are evident, talk of the community vanishing goes too far for Van Dijk. Instead, we should think of a new form of community life, somewhat diffuse, virtual, and on a small scale. In that sense social networks are the opposite of individualization; they connect the smallest elements with each other – "being online may be fully social" (2006, p. 168).[17] New social capital[18] seems to be just as educationally sensitive as many other forms: "more active offline . . . more active online – and vice versa" (Quan-Haase, cited by Van Dijk, 2006, p. 169). In that regard there seems to be a trichotomy rather than a dichotomy – an information elite, the participating majority, and the excluded (p. 185).[19]

To sum up, the network society contains many ambivalences – social expansion (world-wide web) versus reduction (the peer group), colonization of private life versus privatization of public space, inclusion versus exclusion, homogeneity of one's own network versus heterogeneity among clusters, integration versus differentiation, unity versus fragmentation. It is important to acknowledge this duality of the network society, not just to temper exaggerated expectations, but also to avoid cultural pessimism. More information and more communication do not lead to a better or a worse world. They do, however, lead to a different world, one with its own social morphology.[20]

The logic of networks

In order to explore this other world further, let me make an excursion into the science of complex systems. Opinions vary about the legitimacy of such an exercise (Stewart, 2001),[21] yet there are good reasons why the exchange of knowledge between the "hard" and "soft" sciences should be encouraged (Urry, 2003, pp. 16ff.). To begin with, according to Nobel laureate and patriarch of the field Ilya Prigogine, complex systems are valid for all populations showing statistical probability, and that includes humans. In addition, there are many hybrid phenomena in which a distinction between nature and culture is no longer relevant, e.g., health, environment, internet, transportation, and security. The study of complex systems offers the potential to *better understand nodal reality.*[22]

Kees Pieters (2010) made an impressive attempt to develop a *lingua democratica* or language that makes interaction possible among the vocabularies of the different disciplines. "It would seem that complexity itself is becoming the banner that is uniting many islands of science" (Pieters, 2010). He developed a "pattern-oriented approach to complexity," in which patterns (themes of recurring events or objects), feedback (as the core concept of complexity), and uncertainty (as an alternative to chaos) are central. This approach is remarkably similar to my own interpretation of the theory, but has been explicated in the vocabulary of the philosophy of science.[23] I prefer to make my own selection of topics; I discuss structure, synchrony, and stability of networks in that order.

Structures

The logic of networks is of increasing interest in biology, mathematics and the natural sciences, economics, sociology, and the study of organization and governance.[24] In genetic engineering, for example, the *C. elegans* (a tiny nematode) has 20,000 genes; humans have 30,000. That does not seem to be much of a difference, until we realize that the difference is not really in the number of genes, but in the possible relations among them. In these relations, humans are $10^{3{,}000}$ more complex than the miniscule worm (Barabási, 2002, p. 197). This complexity is not an arbitrary piece of data. Relationships within a network are not shared *at random*; they are decided by a network structure. The phenomenal speed at which computer viruses spread, for example, is only understandable because of how networks are ordered.

Some nodes are more important than others simply because they have more links to other nodes. These are *hubs*, or central nodes. Some hubs are connected to other hubs. There are also connectors, which bind one cluster of nodes to another. Computer viruses spread rapidly via hubs and connectors. This network structure was also responsible for the rapid spread of HIV among homosexuals (through a certain number of "hubs" with hundreds of sexual contacts). It also explains why we are connected, via six handshakes, with every other world citizen – the well-known "six degrees of separation."[25]

Networks contain a hidden logic of logarithmic patterns. There are also "scale-free networks," in which there are no underlying gradations. These networks could only be studied properly with the advent of the internet.[26] According to Babarási, "complexity has a strict architecture . . . networks" (2002, p. 7), in which the "truly central position . . . [is] reserved for those nodes that are simultaneously part of many large clusters." These are found in all kinds of systems, from economics to human cells (p. 55f.). This is why every network has its own structure.

Hub formation can only be understood through the phenomenon of "preferential attachments." Every node acquires new links in proportion to its existing links. The more relations it has, the more it will gain. This logarithmic pattern explains how growing networks acquire structure. Other factors also play a role, e.g., the fitness of a node, or "its ability to compete for links." There is competition in networks for links, because more links mean a greater chance of survival. This is also an accepted principle in business – external relations and careful reputation management are important.

Connections between nodes can go in two directions, but usually they go only in one. This simple principle governs how directed networks are formed, which then ultimately develop into clusters, communities, and continents. Network science is increasingly coming to understand networks as structured systems. One talks of stability as the combination of dynamic behavior versus a network's robustness, of tolerance of flaws in the network versus the effectiveness of attacks on it.

A network's robustness is based on hubs and connectors. The potential to switch off hubs selectively makes a network vulnerable. An attack on a terrorist network, for example, would target the hubs (central persons) in an effort to bring it to a point where its survival is under critical threat. Another approach is to starve the hub resources, so that a domino effect or "cascade of failures" occurs (Babarási, 2002, p. 119). Yet there is always the possibility that new networks will form. The most effective way to undermine a network is by offering competing connections that are more attractive and constructive (p. 224). Networks seem to have an inherent structure that allows for a new way of thinking about ordering.

Synchrony

The structures discussed above, which have been discovered in the relatively young science of networks, are built on insights from chaos theory.[27] Meteorologist and mathematician Ed Lorenz discovered that weather forecasts were missing linear causal connections when he entered two almost comparable conditions in his computer (in 1961!). He was shocked to get completely different results. This led to many publications, and ultimately his famous lecture on "predictability," in which he stated that the movement of a butterfly's wing in Brazil could lead to a tornado in Texas (Lorenz, 1979).[28] Many tiny effects from previous events can lead to enormous consequences. Conversely, many disparate elements at a higher level can result in a change in ordering (e.g., the grains of sand in a shifting sand dune). This was the beginning of chaos theory.

A crucial part of chaos theory is the idea that ordering cannot be explained through the behavior of individual elements, but only through their mutually simultaneous activity.[29] This is called synchrony, or "sync" for short (Strogatz, 2003). Why do fireflies light up at the same time and in the same rhythm? How does a flock of starlings move as a single entity? How are glaciers formed, and what are the dynamics of traffic flows?

The phenomenon of synchrony points to oscillators, which can physically or chemically influence each other. Such synchronic activity is everywhere, from the cosmos to our muscles, e.g., in the thousands of cells that keep the heart beating. "At the heart of the universe is a steady, insistent beat: the sound of cycles in sync" (Strogatz, 2003, p. 1).

Such systems are able to organize themselves (Strogatz, 2003, p. 21), and this can be simulated on a computer. A chaotic situation can synchronize and transition to order. This happens in a non-linear manner, so there is no single cause with a single effect. There is a multitude of connections, all acting on one another. This means that, in principle, ordering is unpredictable – there is only a thin line between chaos and order. Order is the result of many interactions that show "a glimpse of some kind of order" (Pieters, 2010, p. 19) on an aggregate level. Between absolute certainty and complete chaos lies a vast area of complexity that can go in many directions.[30] "Synchronized chaos brings us face-to-face with a dazzling new kind of order in the universe, or at least one never recognized before" (Strogatz, 2003, p. 185).

When one oscillator moves another over a critical threshold, they begin to vibrate in sync. This is also evident in human behavior, for example, in traffic patterns, on stock exchanges, at raves and riots, and with singing and clapping. Synchrony seems to be second nature to us (p. 108); we tend to move together (the wave in a football stadium), perhaps even in political landslides. Mark Granovetter (1978) postulated that riots occur when individual decisions are influenced by the behavior of others. If the critical threshold of those present is distributed in series, then after a first vibration (which is always necessary) a person with a critical threshold of 1 joins in, followed by a person with a critical threshold of 2, and so on. This is how a single intention can lead to major consequences.

After a sufficient number of connections there comes a tipping point,[31] which can shift a system quickly. But if the compaction is too great, a second tipping point may be triggered and the phenomenon recedes quickly. An example of this is a fad or craze, which vanishes as quickly as it begins. Traffic flow also has optimal densities. At 35 cars per lane per mile, there is an ordered stream, but a density above or below that leads to a chaotic pattern (Strogatz, 2003, p. 269). This sort of human behavior is relatively involuntary, but most human action is intentional. Free will is not really compatible with directed synchrony;[32] this is why totalitarian regimes use synchrony (p. 273). A science of spontaneous order seems to fit the spirit of the times, as Strogatz suggests (p. 230).

"The propensity to change is the tendency of nature to produce order out of chaos" (Van Dijk, 2006, p. 30). The core idea of order from chaos is that at a certain moment – the critical point – all units in a system act as though they are communicating, although their interactions are strictly local (Watts, 2003). This critical point occurs when there are sufficient long-range connections with a large number of local units, which then organize themselves in clusters (groups, organizations, communities). Small worlds thus become connected to other small worlds. In this way a small unit can set a certain change in motion, which in turn leads to a major transition.

Stability

Network theory has taught us how networks consist of nodes, and these nodes vary in their degrees of importance. Chaos theory has put us on the track of how major orderings or changes can result from small events, and how synchronization with adjacent elements is a decisive factor. Thus we have structure, and we understand how it can organize itself. To fully understand the social ordering in a network society, I regard a third phenomenon as also important. Why is it that structures are not in a permanent state of flux, switching back and forth between chaos and order? How does stability emerge "on the edge of chaos"? The concept of autopoeisis or self-creation is important in understanding this.[33]

In 1961 the Austrian cyberneticist Heinz von Voerster (with G. Pask) published "A predictive model for self-organizing systems." This model introduced the notion that external disturbances can lead to a more orderly structure than before, or "order from noise." It seems counterintuitive – we tend to think that disturbance always causes imbalance. The improved situation, however, emerges through "iterative loops," in which a fixed operation is repeated until a better balance is achieved. This is how a living organism, which is composed of dying cells, is able to reproduce itself. The Chilean biologists Humberto Maturana and Francisco Varela (English edition, 1980) called this phenomenon autopoiesis. Operations within a system flow from a structure built by previous operations.

We are speaking here of relatively closed systems – relative because (in contrast to inanimate matter) they react to the environment. In fact, they continue to adapt as long as their "self-referential mechanism" is not impaired. In other words, systems can change themselves under the influence of external stimuli, but the manner in which structure is determined does not change. Large systems are conditional for each other's evolution. They stimulate one another in a process of stable change. This involves what is called the *thesis of parallelism* – interaction is a synchronic rather than a serial process.

The sociologist Niklas Luhmann and the legal theorist Gunther Teubner have applied autopoiesis to social systems. Luhmann (1990) proposed that individuals tend to reduce complexity by adjusting their expectations. These expectations select and coordinate communication with others. Good collaboration is when an optimal exchange of information about each other's expectations occurs. Luhmann calls the totality of expectations on an aggregated level a social system of the first order (direct interaction between units). With increasing complexity, subsystems of the second order are formed, such as law, morality, religion, and many others. He regards all these subsystems as autopoietic, or self-reproducing. Each subsystem has its own parameter (*modus operandi*) for selecting and reconstructing information based on its expectations.

In the political subsystem, the parameter is the distribution of power; the economy "thinks" in terms of cost-benefit calculations; law is a binary system that makes distinctions between what is and is not right. In this way, systems of social significance are self-organizing according to their core functions. External influences are reconstructed within the system's own structure of meaning. Unless a system crashes completely because of external forces, it can only evolve in a limited sense. This notion can be applied at both the societal and individual level – social and psychological autopoiesis, which we observe in interactions with previously given internal references. Gunther Teubner worked this idea out for the legal system, which has an immanent logic that continually creates new rules of law – the renewal of the system is part of, or even the prerequisite for its continuity.

New clarity

The information era reveals a very different design of social reality. One can argue about the degree to which this is true, and also about how major and severe the consequences may be. Overwrought images should be avoided, and, in my opinion, so should cynical (as opposed to critical) aloofness. Many phenomena in contemporary society can be explained by its networked character; I regard the formal attributes of network logic as important in expanding our understanding. They inspire new insights into the ordering possibilities of networks, including human variants.

We now understand that networks are not unordered totalities of random links or connections between nodes, but that they are built up of structures in which hubs play a central role. Shared systems, clusters, communities, and continents all arise within complex systems. We have also gained some insight into the way changes can occur in networked systems. A small oscillation or situational change can trigger a cascade of changes in an entire system via links with its immediate neighbors. This is how a network, via its hubs, undergoes rapid and radical transformation. This form of change or ordering occurs at the edge of chaos.

This is why I have also focused on the stabilizing principles of systems. A system is capable of a limited amount of change, due to its selective interaction with other systems. Stimuli from the outside lead to reordering and even strengthening of the system, but not to changes within its parameters. The point is that complex forms of ordering can occur because of the structure of networks, the synchrony of operations, and the stability of systems. Let me emphasize that these are only a few examples chosen from the library of complexity theory.

Furthermore, the insights above are purely formal; they lack the moral implications that apply to human networks, and therein lies the distinction between natural and human systems. I am wary of too uncritical an application of natural phenomena to social systems, but at the same time we have learned that chaos can be orderly, if we view it from a different perspective. In the previous section we examined three attempts to organize complexity without direction. In this chapter I have shown that we may be dealing with a new morphology, which allows for a different idea about ordering.

Social ordering can be viewed as a relatively autonomous process, as a logic hiding in the clutter of today's society. It appears when one speaks of the "urgency of problems," the "necessity of dealing with them," and "direction in cooperation." Institutional complexity and lack of moral direction tend to amplify each other. The first results in organizations getting in the way, only wanting to protect their own interests, and being incapable of cooperation.[34] The normative direction needed to achieve a degree of coherence is often absent; this in turn leads to increasing managerial "busyness." Ultimately we need an understanding of what kind of ordering is actually possible and then the ability to steer in that direction. A different perspective gives rise to a new reality.

The tenets of structure, synchrony, and stability are not yet able to yield any insights into the design of human complexity. This new morphology should not make us blind to power struggles, the role of authority, and political opinions about equality and justice; these are important aspects of human society. More specifically, these issues should be regulated by social organization. In the final chapters I examine the ordering principles of human society. Chapter 7 raises the question of how to find normative direction in it. In Chapter 8, I assert that we can regard improvisation as the human version of complexity.

CHAPTER 7

NORMATIVE DIRECTION

Civilizing, providing security, and encouraging citizen participation are the three "programs" in the social ordering offensive. All three arose in the last two decades in the Netherlands, yet they have deep historical roots. There had been other civilizing offensives earlier in the twentieth century (Derksen & Verplanke, 1987), although those initiatives came from the traditional pillars in Dutch society rather than the government. Security – the second program – has traditionally played a major role in the process of nation- and state-building (*pax et securitas*), but in modern societies this is more a question of providing a social safety net. Being a good and active citizen has always been encouraged and promoted, but with the rise of nation-states the emphasis has gradually shifted to a more state-oriented focus.

These three programs could perhaps be better described as a reordering offensive. They are attempts to get a grip on the new conditions in the world without boundaries, which is composed of global and local networks, flows and spaces, and is built of nodes and the links between them. This nodal universe can be understood through new perspectives – network structures, synchrony, and stability based on self-referential principles. And yet, human collectives are not natural systems. People may love or hate each other, they have ideals and value systems, they may believe in God, and some are even prepared to die for him. In our current society, we see undirected rage, a desire for moral direction, and a culture that has little with which one can identify. Together these express the need for ordering and lead to the observation that social ordering cannot be achieved without a normative vertical function in a network society.

The relations in networks should generally be considered as weak. The weak ties in the network society stand in contrast – and sometimes alongside – the strong ties in close-knit communities. Acquaintances stand next to family, a church fellowship next to an internet community, working together in a sports team next to speed dating – strong bonds do indeed play a role, but within loose structures. This enormous variety in the nature of relations – between individuals as well as among organizations – requires a meticulous design of the moral space. Clear prescriptions, prohibitions, permissions, and preferences (Merton's four characteristics; see Chapter 1) are needed, precisely because the variations are so extensive.

In this chapter I consider where the current social ordering can find the materials needed for normative direction; the chapter also deals with the authority that is supposed to give direction. I use "authority" in the broadest sense of the word – the ability to make decisions on the basis of power or prestige.[1] This is an important position reserved for the law, which is a legitimate source for the exercise of power within the framework of the rule of law. We saw (Chapter 6) how the legal system is a stable, self-referential system (autopoiesis) par excellence. I also discussed the direction-giving function that criminal law has brought to the security program (Chapter 4). Yet it is impossible for a society to be based strictly on the law. There are two other normative ordering principles – informal regulation and self-evidence. In this chapter I try to describe the relation between these three principles.

Law without order

Law is currently enjoying unprecedented popularity. In these relatively chaotic times, it is the very institution for us to worry about most. Specifically, criminal law is the subject of political and cultural strife. Increasingly, citizens weigh "the outcomes" of the legal system according to their own sense of justice. Court decisions are no longer necessarily regarded as correct. In conjunction with this, politicians are less inclined to stick to their task as legislators, and are entering the debate on how the law is applied. This popularizing and politicizing of the law indicate our growing social dependence upon it.

Society is leaning more and more on its legal system, and this threatens to crush it. There is pressure from overly high expectations, excessive demands, and the resulting disappointments. Convictions of innocent people by the courts are widely reported in the media, and each and every instance gives the public good reason to doubt the reliability of the justice system. The cases themselves do not interest me here,[2] nor the atmosphere of crisis that surrounds them (Garland, 2001, pp. 19-20, notes the same phenomena in English-speaking nations). What is of interest is the direction of the critique.

The judicial system is not attacked for being too lenient, too slow to respond, or not vigorous enough, but just the opposite. The previously mentioned popularizing and politicizing of these matters takes another direction. Public prosecutors are continually accused of pursuing their activities too vigorously and thus influencing judges on the bench (the Dutch judicial system relies on trial by judges rather than by juries). Confidence or trust in the business of criminal prosecution has two aspects. In the political arena the usual cries are for more and stricter penal interventions. The outrage over wrong decisions by the courts, however, makes it clear that trust in the legal system is also based on the independence of the judge and the legal protection of the defendant. This is not simply a concern for legal scholars, but is an active concern among the populace as well.

Let me confirm the importance of this issue by citing public opinion research. Lünnemann et al. (2008b) conducted a survey among civilians (2,500 citizens via an internet survey, and 54 in 5 focus groups) about the sentencing guidelines of the public prosecution.[3] Participants were asked to rate the seriousness of a variety of offenses, and to grade them on a scale. The research did show some differences between the guidelines and citizens' opinions, but there was a broad consensus. Specifically, victimless crimes were regarded by citizens as less serious (e.g., abusing drugs). Lünnemann and her colleagues also found no indications that citizens would be more punitive than professional judges.[4]

Lünnemann et al. (2008a) also studied meetings between citizens and representatives of public prosecutors' offices. The citizens did not seem to have a realistic grasp of what public prosecutors' offices actually do. Many personal experiences were shared and the meetings as such were appreciated. The issue was more a question of ignorance, rather than a difference in insight. Citizens perceive the law as alien, and tend to take a less dogmatic approach to justice than scholars do. At the same time, people shy away from the consequences of such an approach, namely, the introduction of lay law. In qualitative research on the perception of the legal system (Boutellier & Lünnemann, 2007), emotion and objectivity were recurring elements in respondents' narratives. Wrong judgments were experienced as disappointing, or even as a personal affront. The judicial system is supposed to be impartial.

The conclusions citizens draw from such experiences are ambivalent. On the one hand, the authoritarian vertical position of criminal law is not accepted; on the other hand, people are not really ready to abandon it. In the study cited, only one person (out of approximately fifty respondents) was in favor of direct influence by laypersons on the outcome of criminal proceedings. This leads to an important finding – the judge may not be trusted, but fellow citizens are trusted even less! It makes sense to consider the position of the administration of justice in relation to "the law," as it is understood in psychoanalysis (Maruna et al., 2004). The judge can be seen as representing social order; this makes it possible for the citizen, as a subject of the law, to perceive him- or herself as an independent identity (Cleiren, 2008).

The law represents protection, inviolability, and a superior capacity for judgment. Such a system is highly valued, yet at the same time it seems as though it is not responsive enough to personal needs and desires. Protection *and* empathy are wanted: an objective authority that is also communicative, a superior power of judgment with sensitivity to what is happening. What is wanted is a human, empathic judge who is nevertheless neutral and objective. People want an approachable legal system, without having to be part of it. They want to feel it is "their law" that is being pronounced. As one respondent said, "I like the fiction that the law represents us all, our kind of state, the community we want to have" (Boutellier & Lünnemann, 2007, p. 10).

The legal system is, ideally, the objectivized expression of moral order in society. The law forms both the expression and the codification for that which is regarded as necessary and desirable. It draws its ultimate legitimacy from its enforcement. Citizens are willing to abide by the law when they know that it protects them. This virtual social contract (discussed by the philosophers of the Enlightenment) came under pressure at the end of the twentieth century. The time when the law could be called "a peaceful possession"[5] is far behind us; it is now the terrain of political and cultural conflict. And yet the legal system can only generate trust within a context of self-regulation. The law should be carried out through civil ordering, so if the legal system needs an underlying moral order, what should that look like?

Order without law

To put this question of moral order radically – is order without law possible? The lawyer Robert C. Ellickson thinks so, or so it seems from the title of his book *Order without law* (1991). Ellickson thinks that more spontaneous order arises without law than is generally assumed. He is against the Hobbesian idea that only law, and the power of the state on which it is based, can create order. Social order emerges through various forms of behavior regulation, of which the law is only one. Sociologically that is more or less self-evident (Wrong, 1995), but Ellickson's studies teach us a great deal about the empirical relation between formal and informal systems.

Ellickson researched conflicts about livestock in rural Shasta County, California – damage caused by livestock, cattle theft, conflicts about grazing rights, and the like. At first blush, these situations do not seem to be relevant to the urban issues in our society, but his study is more concerned with the structure of conflict resolution than the nature of the conflicts. Shasta County has "close-knit groups," or relatively closed, homogeneous communities. He found that most problems in these communities were resolved using informal norms and various forms of conflict resolution – order without law indeed.

Ellickson formulated the following hypothesis: "members of a close-knit group develop and maintain norms whose content serves to maximize the aggregate welfare that members obtain in their workaday affairs without one another" (p. 167). In other words, there is a strong utilitarian ethos in cohesive communities that determines how daily conflicts are resolved. He argues this theory of optimal utility in relation to economic and sociological approaches to the law, and places the law within a larger framework of regulation. This in turn brings us to the results in game theory from Axelrod and others, which looked at optimal forms of cooperation – for example, the well-known "prisoner's dilemma."

The most rational strategy in such situations is "tit-for-tat," if the other chooses a non-cooperative strategy. Ellickson discovers an ingenious system for social ordering from this perspective that is based on two sorts of sanctions, five controlling authorities, and five sorts of rules. Sanctions can be divided into positive, rewarding reactions, and negative, punishing reactions ("carrots and sticks"). In principle, rewards are given for pro-social behavior, and punishments for antisocial behavior. "Normal" behavior – in both a statistical and normative sense – is in principle ignored. This casual observation by Ellickson is crucial for my explorations, as will be seen below. After all, normal behavior presupposes and feeds social trust.

In principle, interventions in Shasta County are chosen based on what seems likely to give the best outcome; social ordering arises through maximizing utility. The choice between using informal regulation (as social power) and the law (as government intervention) is often difficult. The specifics of the conflict and the parties involved play a decisive role. Ellickson differentiates the social distance between the parties, the size and nature of the stakes involved, and the possibility of shifting the costs to a third party. Agencies, sanctions, and regulations together form a complete and complex system that ultimately determines social order. The formal justice system only plays a role if social forces fail to correct or resolve, or, in other words, the stakes involved are too high.

Ellickson acknowledges that "order without law" is more difficult in larger communities, and especially in nation-states. Even stronger, the lack of cohesion in current civil society is precisely part of the problem. Apart from this empirical relativization, there is also a political-normative problem. Maximizing general utility for one group can come at the expense of others on the outside, or those who are not part of the group. There are always normative perspectives – justice, equality, freedom – that cannot be understood in (merely) utilitarian terms. Maximizing utility is thus a limited moral criterion. "From both positive and normative perspectives, norms have their limits and law has its place," is how Ellickson sums up the relation between formal law and social regulation (p. 283).

Although the title of his book suggests otherwise, Ellickson concludes that ultimately a just social order is not possible without a formal legal system. However, if the importance of the informal social order is ignored, we risk creating a world with more law and less order, according to the last sentence in his book. Formal law and informal regulation both presuppose and strengthen each other. But the question is whether these suffice. "Normal" behavior in Ellickson's analysis is of secondary importance. His focus is on the resolution of conflicts. The moral space does indeed find its boundaries through legal proceedings, informal conflict resolution, punishment, and/or the enforcement that proceeds from them. Yet it is primarily determined through everyday behavior in which interventions are not necessary. That is the importance of social trust.

The domain of the self-evident

One speaks of putting trust in the economy, in the government, in the police, in the courts, in each other. Trust is a commodity, a good; it has a positive value, and political and social institutions do all they can to gain people's trust (e.g., Meurs, 2008). Current social science literature is overflowing with "trust," which is being studied in a variety of disciplines – economics, sociology, political science, and public administration studies. Trust is a popular concept in many disciplines. There are psychological, communitarian, and institutional dimensions of trust, according to the literature, which are associated with a variety of primary sources.

The general *psychological* attitude[6] points to upbringing. The basic feeling that "others should behave the way they want to be treated" has deep existential roots; according to Bo Rothstein (1992, 2000) it precedes any civil engagement. *Communitarian* trust, as emphasized by Robert Putnam (1992, 2000), can be found in the social bonds of people brought together in community activities and affairs. *Institutional* trust refers to experiences with institutions that treat you in the manner you want to be treated. Trust is thus a broad concept that has many sources, but what is it really good for?

In his book *Trust* (1995), Francis Fukuyama emphasizes its economic value. The rational calculator – the prototype of *homo economicus* – is joined by the moral man. Trust is closely related to shared norms and values, and is crucial for a functioning economy. Especially in a network society, the willingness to cooperate and to share information is crucial. In organizational sociology trust is regarded as one of the central factors in successful cooperation (Bijlsma-Frankema & Costa, 2005). This applies both to trust within the organization as well as trust among organizations. Trust is regarded as a necessary counterweight to competition for successful operations (Fukuyama, 1995).

Besides the economic stakes regarding trust, increasing attention is given to its relation to democracy. Robert Putnam gave this discussion impetus with his work on trust as social capital. His book *Bowling alone* (2000; previously the title of an article) deals with the erosion of social relations in American society. Putnam shows at great length how associations and clubs, volunteer work, and social activities are declining, and this undermines the moral, social, and political quality of the community. Americans are, so to speak, bowling alone more and more. His book is a warning to civil society – a vital democracy needs a strong sense of community, as he showed earlier in his analysis of northern and southern Italy (Putnam et al., 1992).

The argument is familiar. Social relations promote trust. In a world without boundaries the number of meaningful relationships declines, and specifically those based on voluntary connections (clubs, associations, and the like). To explain this, Putnam refers to the lack of involvement by younger generations, the undermining influence of television, increased mobility, and decreased social time. His analysis, of course, attracted substantial criticism – the numbers didn't add up, the causal relations were contested, and the interpretations were unsound. Imrat Verhoeven (2009, pp. 41ff.) also contested the relevance of a similar decrease in social contact and trust for Dutch society. The key issue here, however, is the role of trust in the social ordering process, and that cannot be disputed.

For this reason I regard trust as an important complement to the law and informal regulation, as discussed by Ellickson, especially for dealing with spontaneous interactions that do not need to be regulated or are implicit (e.g., family relations). Such spontaneous interactions take place in what I would call the *domain of the self-evident* (see in this regard Komter, 2003). Social order needs the law and informal types of regulating or maximizing utility, but ordering needs a third factor – self-evident interaction – in order to be successful. This goes beyond momentous experiences. Rothstein (2000) introduced the term "collective memories" – who are we, who are the others, and what happens if and when we trust each other? Trust is also rooted in a shared past.

Collective memory is particularly relevant to development in post-socialist countries, where citizens' trust in the government and institutions must be rebuilt. Negative collective memory is a real stumbling block to social trust in such situations. Rothstein uses this idea of collective memory in contrast to the instrumentalist-rationalist approach of game theory, which

Ellickson also used. In Rothstein's opinion, trust is more than the result of "give and take."[7] This is not the place to discuss the finer points of the ontology of trust. Let me just note that self-evidence is crucial for stable relations between (government) institutions, networks, and individuals.

Control and trust

Law, informal regulation, and self-evident interaction are three dynamics of social ordering. They determine the authority with which direction can be given in societal complexity. There is so much more that can be said about them that I treat them here with discretion, my main purpose being to show that the necessary function of authority can take various forms in a network society. In this section I look at how they relate to the nodal universe discussed in Chapter 6, including network logic, the complexity of structure, synchrony that makes communality possible, and self-regulation (autopoiesis) that achieves stability. These approaches, however, say nothing about the quality of relations in social networks. In a manner of speaking, natural phenomena are "morally neutral."

According to Barabási, "To describe society we must dress the links of the social network with actual dynamical interactions between people" (2002, p. 225). Referring to these interactions, many quote an article by Granovetter from 1973 (long before the discovery of the concept of the network society) in which he noted the increasing importance of "weak ties." I have already pointed this out. Close-knit communities have strong bonds that are based on tradition, self-evident authority, and obedience. Modern communal bonds are looser and are based on dynamic rather than static interactions. Such relations are more dominant than ever – not only between individuals, but also among organizations. The strong bond within the traditional social pillars has been replaced with looser, more functional bonds among organizations.

How is it possible to achieve reliability when relations are not based on tradition, authority, and obedience? I propose that the reliability of weak bonds can be realized by two methods

– control and trust. Control is founded on formal law, and, in a milder form, informal regulation. Relations are regulated by the law, rules, contracts, covenants, and informal norms. In the shadow of the law (and, if need be, enforced by it) is a growing world of surveillance, regulation, and auditing, which is motivated by the desire to avoid losing control (Power, 1994, 2007).

Besides these forms of control we have self-evident interactions based on trust. Trust has many sources – authority, culture, religion, shared experience, communal memories, values and norms, the common good, and normal personal contact. In a network society, trust is not guaranteed by strong bonds of kinship or closed communities. When one does not want to rely on forms of control, then personal contact and social capital are options; these can be regarded as networking skills.[8] The greatest benefit of reliable behavior is trust that others will also behave well. This is why Komter (2003) sees reciprocity as the moral key to modern society.

It would be naïve to believe in a world based simply on trust, yet a world based on nothing but control is unappealing and probably not even possible. Control and trust can be seen as the moral parameters of a network society.[9] Therein lies the authority of normative direction. As for patterns of obedience to it, there are in principle three possibilities.[10] Exercise of authority can be legitimized and accepted, given voluntary assent in a specific normative setting. This applies to almost all power relations in an institutional context, and the pattern is also visible in modern relations within work situations. This is more a question of the distribution of roles rather than fundamentally unequal positions. Of course, the degree of one's voluntary participation is subject to bargaining. As this becomes less, then the second form comes into play.

Exercise of authority can also be based on a clearly delineated functional power relationship. This applies to families, schools, and all relationships in which dependence is inherent in the function of the institution. This form of obedience is also visible in more traditional work relations. An obvious example is the army, whose functioning depends on hierarchy. Another extreme situation is the prison – one's position determines the nature of the relationship. The potential for abuse of power is a characteristic of these situations, because there is almost no possibility of escape.[11] Finally, obedience to authority can be compelled. Such obedience relationships are in principle not legitimate and as such are criminal; examples include human trafficking and other exploitative situations.

Vertical relations are thus admittedly part of the network society, but they are not structurally internalized. They require the assent of the parties involved, or they are clearly delineated; if not, then they are criminal. Ultimately everybody has the right to speak, and opportunities for expression are more plentiful than ever. This situation of equality, which is a hallmark of modernity, has become radicalized in the network society. This is why people often have difficulty in establishing or maintaining a relation of authority.[12] This can be seen in relations between parents and children, but also between teachers and students, and managers and employees. Classic situations of obedience are in decline, and new forms of authority need to be found.

The hybrid authority of government

A network's continuity lies in the balance between control and trust, creating structure, synchrony, and stability. They ultimately determine the degree of authority with which a network can operate, both externally and internally. This arrangement raises the question of the meaning of political and administrative authority – on what is it based? Maarten Hajer (2009) researched this brilliantly, based on three cases – the murder of Theo van Gogh, the rebuilding of Ground Zero, and the British mad cow disease crisis. Authority in politics is never self-evident, but should be earned, or, to use Hajer's term, *enacted* (both determined and staged). Governing, according to Hajer, is first and foremost about the authoritative determination of meanings. Politics revolves around this struggle. Authority is not an attribute of persons, but of communication: "finding a way to speak in meaningful terms" (2009, p. 12). In a media-driven world, dramatization is increasingly important, preferably as (personal) conflict.

Classic government is based on territorial order, with interlocking institutions, a clear distinction between politicians and the bureaucracy, legitimized through elections, supported by policy research, in the hope of public participation, and with the media as the messenger. These seven hallmarks laid the foundation of the administrative authority of the nation-state. Because of the changed position of the state (see Chapter 3 above), classic government falls short in its power to implement, its legitimacy, and its ability to learn (the traditional governance cycle is disturbed by permanent interaction and influence (Hajer, 2009, pp. 29ff.)). This gives rise to the new "network governance," or policy above, below, and alongside established bonds.

There are no self-evident rules any more, and policy must be continually renegotiated. Hajer calls this the "institutional void," which leads to ambiguity.[13] The manner in which parties reach agreement also contributes to the result: "negotiated governance" (p. 35). Authority arises from the credibility achieved through this process: "network governance involves a continuous back and forth between improvised settings of negotiation and established settings of accountability." In practice there can be simultaneous forms of both classic and networked governance, in which the degrees of effectiveness, legitimacy, and fairness play a role (Fung and Wright's "empowered participatory governance"; see Chapter 5 above).

One problem with this "network policy" is that the media continue to reason from the classic paradigm, because it better fits their motto of "politics is drama." According to Hajer, a new idea of authority is needed, framed in terms of "the string of enactments that create and sustain authority" (p. 179). Classic government is part of network governance, in which a more personal style of enacting policy is preferred. An example of this "new policy" is the "regime change" that occurred in Rotterdam after the 2002 elections. I borrow this term from Pieter Tops (2007), who took it from Clarence Stone (1989). Stone developed a theory of municipal regimes: new cooperative bonds that he analyzed in his study of Atlanta. He also uses complexity as his starting point, and notes that, often without traditional "command power," structures manage to form various arrangements based on shared goals among the interested parties.

A municipal regime is "an informal but relatively stable coalition of actors from inside and outside the municipal administration, who pool their powers based on shared perspectives and interests, and thereby can give direction to the development of the municipal community" (Tops, 2007, p. 23). They consist of *a broad coalition* which is based on *an overarching agenda*, sufficient *resources* for execution, and the formation of *an alignment* (getting all their ducks in a row). Then the coalition can carry out municipal policy programs. Stone distinguishes between strong and weak regimes; the first still have a chain of command, the second have more of a network structure.

Tops analyzed the situation in Rotterdam after the murder of the populist politician Pim Fortuyn, which he regarded as a "regime change." "How a municipal administration reinvented itself" was the subtitle of his book. In March 2002, Fortuyn's party Livable Rotterdam (*Leefbaar Rotterdam*) received almost 40 percent of the votes in one election. In the Dutch multiparty system, this was a clarion call for one of the largest ordering programs for safety in recent decades. Tops describes in detail the actors, the deliberations, and the actions that gave form to the policy for security. It succeeded,[14] according to Tops, thanks to the combination of active implementation in the "front line" and tight management that targeted effective interventions.

In fact, Tops thinks there was a classic government model. It was not so much a rational management plan, but rather organizing the "power to act." The core of the package was execution, rather than the existing structure. This is obvious from the "triangle of opportunity" – the mayor, an external adviser, and the energetic head of the security project office, who led the process. Two traditional triangle partners (the police commissioner and the chief prosecutor) were in the second tier. Tops (2007, p. 30) points out that the "networking of management" needs a supporting narrative, or an organizing concept in which both the fragmented network society and the classic hierarchy can be conceived.

Rotterdam's security policy is a good example of the combination of classic government and nodal management as described by Hajer. Managerial authority by necessity has a hybrid character. Exaggerated ideas about network control and working horizontally fail to appreciate the need for ordering, which unfolds in human society as more or less authoritarian, regulated, and controlled. In a complex society without direction, one organizes ordering with an optimal alignment of the participating actors. A communal goal or dramatic theme (security!) is essential here, as well as agreement about the roles of the various actors and the fine-tuning of the reliability of each of them, based on supervision and control or through the creation of mutual trust (reciprocity).

Horizontal and vertical relations

Reflections on the world without boundaries often make reference to horizontal relations – a flat world, according to Thomas Friedman (2005), in particular with an eye to the globalizing economy. That fits with the image of eroding structures of vertical authority. Terms such as atomizing and anomie are used; individuals are supposed to be more independent and that requires new forms of community. (That was the motive behind Balkenende's civilizing "defensive.") The network society's social morphology, however, differs from the individual versus the collective. It is about relations in networks, which can be little/big, local/global, narrow/open, controlled/trust-inspiring, and all at the same time.

We can think of complexity in terms of network structures, synchrony, and self-organization, but human networks also have a moral component. They are formed in a moral space, which is composed of the totality of rules and expectations that determine human relations. In this chapter I have delineated the components of this space in law, informal regulation, and trust. Even three-dimensional networks have a top and a bottom

(Van Dijk, 2006), as well as a left and a right, and a before and an after. In other words, horizontal and vertical have not disappeared, but their structure in networks is much less static. Relations can even be diagonal.

Nodes and clusters of nodes are always connected with other networks, in which they play other roles. The nature of the relations within an institutional network is determined (among other things) by the function of a given node. In general, one can posit that, in horizontal networks, network relations are tuned and regulated ad hoc. In vertical relations, the tendency to regulate and control is stronger. "The steeper, the stricter" could be a rule of thumb, and vice versa. What is at stake plays a major role. In life-or-death situations, abilities, responsibilities, and their control are critical. The reliability of the actors must be guaranteed. The operating room is not a proper venue for negotiations, and the same applies to disaster management, crisis situations, and wrong-doing. Police work also usually demands direct action within a legal framework, strict protocols, and frequently-reviewed work policies.

The tendency to regulate is also strong when serious financial or social interests are involved. We learned from the financial crisis of 2008 that regulation of major interests can be insufficient, if it is based on the idea that the system can self-regulate. The market managed to secure regulation for itself in a strongly neoliberal atmosphere in the 1990s, which fostered trust in the market's capacities to self-regulate, and pushed back government regulation. This shows that the level of regulation is a politically contentious topic that exposes strong ideological differences.

Various authors argue in favor of common sense when it comes to the nature and quality of the network society. The rule of law and institutions are still standing, even though their positions have shifted. At the same time we must recognize that the world without boundaries has a complex palette of organizations that both overlap and are separate, are independent and dependent, and which are more or less communicating elements, clusters, and communities. Human complexity needs the direction that can be found in the law, in social regulation, or in what can be seen as self-evident. These offer the basis for control and trust in the collaborative practices of networks.

That does not, however, cover all that can be said about social ordering in a world without boundaries. To transcend complexity without direction, I seek a mechanism that explains how we can live in a society we find chaotic but still inhabitable, even if only in our own way. The ideologically inspired ordering of the twentieth century led to the welfare state, which was top-heavy and apparently unsustainable. This situation morphed into a sacred belief in the ordering ability of the market. In the triad of state, market, and community, the last is now first again. How can we possibly even think about the community if we don't believe in it? That is the subject of the next chapter.

CHAPTER 8

THE IMPROVISING SOCIETY

In this book I have used a variety of words to characterize society. Each has a slightly different accent, yet they are all appropriate. The "network society" refers to the infrastructure of nodes (individuals and organizations) and the relations among them. The "information society" points to the technological conditions for networks. A "world without boundaries" indicates the global dimensions of current society. As for the precise causal relations between globalization, information technology, and the growth of networks, let's just say they are remarkably complex.

I bring these together in the concept of the "improvising society" to reflect and clarify the ordering process in this complexity without direction. "Improvising" seems to capture the essence of how we organize a world without boundaries – with the proviso that the normative function is also included. In this final chapter, I examine its sustainability and the consequences of this characterization. The comparison between society and playing music has been made before, as has the comparison with jazz. It is often used in social psychology and management studies which also has a strongly implied normative message – "this is how we should live."[1]

I am thinking of a sociological meaning that has to do with society's actual organization – "this is how we live." Now the combination of the words "improvisation" and "organization" seems to create an oxymoron. The heart of improvisation always seems to be spontaneity; one thinks of the soloist freely conjuring music from an instrument as if by magic, yet this is a limited representation of what is happening (e.g., Kernfield, 1995). The soloist's spontaneity takes place within the context of his/her fellow musicians, the key in which the music is played, its theme, motif, progressions, intro, and finish.

In an even broader context, the soloist must take into account the instruments, acoustics, stage setting, the public, as well as previous experiences, memories, and aesthetic preferences (Cobussen, 2009). In other words, that spontaneity is embedded in a larger framework, and the heart of improvisation shifts from spontaneity to *fine-tuning*. A successful improvisation comes into being through the fine-tuning of all these factors in the environment, experience, and consonance of playing together. Fine-tuning implies structure, synchrony, and self-organization. It creates ordering among identities, which I regard as the essence of the social ordering process.[2] This insight makes it possible to reflect further, perhaps even speculatively, on social institutions and their politics.

Improvisation as social representation

Charles Taylor (2004) introduced the concept "social imaginaries" in a book with the same title. These are the representations we need to make the everyday practices of a society possible: "the ways people imagine their social existence, how they fit together with others, how things go on between them and their fellows, the expectations that are normally met, and the deeper normative notions and images that underlie these expectations" (p. 23). They are more than ideas or attitudes; they are the basic concepts of social order, "an implicit understanding." Characteristic of Western society are the ideas of modern society as a market, a public sphere, and a form of autonomy.

There is no place in our concepts of society for a God or higher power that steers us all, as there was in the pre-modern era. Taylor (a practicing Catholic) describes this transition in *A secular age* (2007), in which he painstakingly shows how the hierarchically ordered world of the Middle Ages gradually lost its enchantment and became a secular constitutional state. In that process, three tasks were accomplished – the disciplining of personal life, an ordered society, and an inner attitude that is self-sufficient (Taylor, 2007, p. 82f.). We have bound ourselves together in a social contract of rights and responsibilities, which since the Enlightenment has led to an instrumental representation in which "security and prosperity [are] the principal goals" (Taylor, 2004, p. 13).

Security and prosperity are thus seen as the comprehensive goals of Western society, to be realized in the absence of an internalized hierarchy. Our "sociality" is based on ideas of mutual profit, organized by a political state, under the conditions of freedom and equality (Taylor, 2004, p. 19f.). These ideas and the accompanying practices should be constantly re-calibrated and re-verified. Every era gives rise to ideas that fit the prevailing conditions. Currently, according to Taylor, we are dealing with a "radical horizontality" – every member of society has immediate access to the whole. This places new demands on our imagination.

We should see ourselves as part of horizontal (I would like to say "three-dimensional") collective actions, and our society as a system of processes. In the simultaneous presence of everything and everybody, one realizes the meaning we have for each other (Taylor, 2004, chapter 11). With this image, Taylor opens a new relational perspective on the network society. He postulates competencies in terms of clarity, openness, transparency, synchrony, selection, and transactions. These are skills, but they also refer to the need and willingness to participate in a complex of processes, in which some coherence is necessary.

Coherence is achieved both willingly and unwillingly – willingly, when the actors participate voluntarily in collective actions, unwillingly when they have to be commanded from above. Of key importance in "the process" is the calibration or fine-tuning of one's own activity with others in the immediate environment, who in turn also experience themselves as part of a larger environment. This gets to the essence of what I call the improvising society. It is the totality of tuning processes in the area in which the social order of the world without boundaries is formed.

This is different from a hierarchical society, in which the processes are not only imposed from above, but are also internalized as such. This does not mean that the improvising society no longer has a "top-down" structure. Human social order presupposes normativity; I explained that in detail in the previous chapter. Many actual processes have fixed structures, rules, and protocols. It is also possible that networks generate sufficient trust, based on reciprocity, tuning, and personal contact.

Herman van Gunsteren (2006) argues in favor of working from the results of the democratic process, rather than fixating on the chaotic process that precedes it. According to him, democracy is "order without a boss," and we should trust in its self-organizing capability: "because of the impossibility of direct and comprehensive control, trust becomes a core element of self-organization" (p. 60). Although I make a similar argument, I regard this as too naïve a guideline for policy. The ordering programs I described in Part Two show the importance of normative direction in human networks. Control (based on law and regulation) *and* trust form the guiding parameters for the order of improvisation.

A little divertimento on improvisation[3]

According to the dictionary, improvisation is a vocal or instrumental performance that is played at the same moment it is composed; it also refers to variations on a familiar theme or subject. Improvisation has the added meaning of working with what is available at that particular moment – as the Dutch say, you have to row with the oars you've got. Improvisation is most often used in theater and music. In improvisational theater, or improv, actors make up the story, the characters, and the dialog on the spot. Awareness, listening, focusing, trusting, and instinctive or spontaneous acting are all important skills for improv actors. However, improvisation usually brings to mind music, and jazz in particular.

Musical improvisation is the spontaneous formation of melody, which takes place in a specific harmony and a given rhythm. Both the spontaneous nature and the structure have a musicological history. The simplest musical form is linear – the melody. Gregorian chant, originally monophonic, was richly embellished in the early Middle Ages – specific vowels in the text were elongated and spread over clusters of notes, which gave the effect of improvisation. Polyphony began to develop in the eighth century, first from two parallel voices, then four. This reached its apex in the contrapuntal music of the Renaissance, a complex polyphonic texture of melodies and countermelodies. The second half of the sixteenth century saw the introduction of songs with chordal accompaniment, or harmony.

Starting in the seventeenth century (the Baroque era) harmonic accompaniment was introduced through chording on the harpsichord, which together with a viola da gamba, cello, or bassoon formed the *basso continuo* or figured bass. The melody was embellished with trills and arpeggios, which were forms of improvisation. Bach, for example, was an outstanding improviser (just listen to his organ toccatas). Between 1770 and 1800, more written variations on melody, harmony, and rhythm appeared, as well as the cadenza, or concluding ornamental passage. Improvisation returned with the rise of Romanticism (Liszt, for example), or music composed and written as though it were improvised.

Improvisation is very common in jazz, and usually takes place melodically around a set group of chords. In early jazz (beginning of the twentieth century), improvisation did not venture far from the set melody and was more about embellishment. Polyphonic improvisations usually involve variations on the melody. Barry Kernfield (1995) distinguishes between "paraphrasic" improvisation (embellishing), "formulaic" improvisation (combining fragments into something new), and "motivic" improvisation (working around a motif). Improvisation is spontaneous, in other words, it takes place in relation to something else.

Kernfield also points out that in jazz the differences between composing, arranging, and improvising are blurred: "the key issue is control, what to compose and what to leave open" (p. 99). An arrangement is a written free form – a temporary ordering – based on a commanding melody (motif). Improvisation makes use of fixed elements – riffs, repetitive motifs against a changing harmonic background. There are also completely free forms of jazz improvisation, in which the harmonies (the chords) are also improvised. In free jazz, usually nothing is fixed in advance. At its core, improvisation is a form of instant composing, in which the composition is determined by the interaction with the other players, the environment, the musical history, and the internal coherence of the music.

Technically speaking, this coherence is defined by vertical moments in horizontal flows. The chord is vertical. A distinction is made between the sub- and superstructure with chord anchors. Between the chords there are also resonances, transitional notes, or alternating tones, which create moments of surprise. Consonances and dissonances are sounded; a dissonance is preferably followed by a resolution. The melody and harmony come together in the music's measure, thus creating the rhythm. Usually there are excursions and returns, with the root or tonic chord as the starting point for progression. The tonic, dominant, and subdominant chords are strongly related and form the harmonic organization of the composition.

All this applies to improvised music as well. One usually talks about improvisation based on harmonic structure, unless a deliberate choice is made not to use it, as in free jazz. Even then, however, there is no getting around the environment, history, the distinctive characteristics of the instruments, and the expectations of the audience, which are of particular importance. Current expectations tend more to the rhythmic than the harmonic, along lines of tension and resolution. Improvisation determines the form and direction of the composition. Yet it is not free – it is bound to vertical moments of synchrony between melody, harmony, meter, and rhythm. Successful improvisation is achieved through harmonic and metric coherence (or undermines that deliberately). Jazz is organized freedom; improvisation presupposes smart organization.

Harmonization and how to organize it

The organization of improvisation as a societal process, scientifically speaking, refers to the enormous terrain of governance and managerial sciences. Since the 1950s, these disciplines have gradually acquired a central role in the social sciences. This can be understood as the scientific answer to the problem of complexity without direction. The issues dealt with include the relations between public and private organizations, kinds of leadership, the role of values, control of networks, organizational integrity, the relation between policy and governance, and between governance and organization.

Governance is a key concept in the literature of the previous decades. The word itself has dozens of definitions. Burris et al. (2008, p. 9) defined it as "organized efforts to manage the course of events in a social system," and devoted a two-page footnote to it. In the context of this book, I prefer a simpler definition – "the organization of fine-tuning." *Governance* is obviously related to *government*; it has emerged because government gradually lost its monopoly on public problems (Burris et al., 2008).

Yet it is about more than the question of how public and private actors should relate to each other. Governance is closely related to issues that are regarded as *wicked problems*. Such problems have no definitive answers because of their great complexity, continually changing conditions, and ambiguous ideas about what might be good approaches to solutions (Van Steden, 2010). Van Delden (2009) speaks in a similar vein about "poisonous problems," which complicate policy-making, let alone policy implementation. As Klijn and Koppenjan (1994, p. 148) baldy put it, it is the observation that "policy comes into being in a complex interaction of processes among a large number of actors."

The literature on governance abounds with rather indigestible research on conditions, forms, stages, and relations, all of which is meant to provide insight into the most effective and efficient work methods. Van Delden's research on chain collaboration in numerous areas (security, youth care, culture, work, and incomes) has been most relevant to my research because it shows the importance of how collaboration is developed. He found two forms of stagnation – sham collaboration and island collaboration. The most important finding in the context of the improvising society is that it is behavioral impulses rather than interests which influence the parties involved.

Van Delden distinguishes between intentional impulses, which mainly have to do with the conditions under which a network functions, activist impulses, which are geared to short-term results, and finally binding impulses, which aim to achieve sustainable results. These impulses, which come respectively from government, professionals, and managers, can obviously conflict with each other. This kind of stagnation leads to negotiation in which mutual give-and-take, peer relations, and vertical coordination are crucial for completion. "The power of collaboration is to be found in the energy of behavioral impulses" (Van Delden, 2009, p. 93). This is exactly what typifies improvisation.

Van Delden contrasts two strategies. The exploratory strategy focuses on the interaction between actors in a high-profile situation, which can generate serious impact on major local differences. The programmatic strategy sets clear goals and an implementation program, and usually has less impact, but also fewer disparities. Obviously there are many possibilities in between these two; we might call them "mixed enterprises" (see Nederland et al., 2009). We recognize the difference between the classic modern and the networked governances of Hajer (Chapter 7). And we see the sliding scale between improvisation, arrangement, and composition. "In the thousands of collaborative bonds in almost all sectors there is a gradual transformation toward a networked public services" (Van Delden, 2009, p. 142). I call it the improvising society.

Between incident and institution

This brings up the question of the events around which the fine-tuning takes place. We might call them "attractors," as in complexity theory. An attractor is a state in which a system organizes itself over time. In principle there are three possibilities for "turning on" the social ordering process – incidents, initiatives, and centers of gravity.

Incidents are defined by their contingencies – they simply arise and can lead to ad-hoc actions, regulation, or even structural measures. For example, disturbances by youth in the Amsterdam district of Slotervaart became frequent enough to result in steps being taken. The parties involved ranged from the police and youth workers to housing associations and the school system.[4] We also see a programmatic formation of order in safe houses, and physical partnerships around security problems (Ministerie van Justitie, 2009b). Incidents create a sense of urgency, which in turn triggers further actions in a more or less systematic way.

Initiatives are intentional actions by individual nodes (persons or organizations) that can ultimately provide direction for an entire network. One resident gets an entire neighborhood involved in cleaning up; one activist can bring about large-scale demonstrations. It is precisely in a complex situation that individual citizens can play a crucial role as "everyday makers" (Bang & Sørensen, 1999). Organizations (sometimes mediated by an active fellow worker) can also take the lead in partnerships and networks. Initiatives are closely related to Van Delden's "behavioral impulses."

Centers of gravity, finally, can be conceived of as organizations or institutions that matter the most in certain policy areas.[5] They can be hubs (nodes with many connections), but also centers of power or expensive physical facilities. They create fields of activity through governance, but also through preventive intervention. The criminal justice system, for example, as the *ultimum remedium*, has grown to include crime prevention, risk management, and precaution (see the securitization process in Chapter 5). Criminal justice is thus a center of gravity in the field of security.[6] In healthcare, specialist services occupy a similar position. A field of preventive activities and risk management comes into existence to avoid having to call on specialists.

The incident creates the urgency, the individual the initiative, and the center of gravity the field. The ordering comes into being more or less arbitrarily – it emerges. When the aim is programmatic ordering, the attractors that can function as the dynamic nucleus need to be appointed. And this observation points to the institutional significance of the improvising society. What remains of a society if we cannot envision it other than in terms of networks and their tuning patterns? Is there even any reason to use the word "society"?

The answer to this question can be found in the gravity and coherence of institutional organization, in which the nation state set the political boundaries. Ordering based on fine-tuning around incidents, initiatives, and centers of gravity takes place in relatively stable fields such as healthcare, security, education, and all other public and private sectors. The fine-tuning within and among institutions arises from the centers of gravity of the relevant institutional practices. These are to be found in each institution's core function, which gives direction to the field in which it functions. The core function determines the identity of the organization.[7]

In my opinion, the core of education, for example, is the *transfer* of knowledge and life experience from one generation to another. The educational system defines itself through this core function. This determines the curriculum, but also, in social terms, implies a generational difference, a degree of order in the class, and reciprocal respect for the roles of teacher and student.[8] A substantive core practice for, e.g., a juvenile correction facility is *moral correction*, or the explicit rejection of delinquent behavior and the attempt to effect a moral rethinking in the youths involved.

Another example of a substantive core is *empathetic support* in healthcare; in this context Moll (2006) speaks of "doctoring." Caring for one's fellow humans is inconceivable without the capacity for empathy that is principally directed at supporting those in need of care. The core of police work can be conceived of as *preserving normative boundaries*, both through public order and through the criminal justice system – or, in everyday speech, enforcement (Boutellier, 2010). The list could continue – the Ministry of Justice is at its core about *proportionate retribution*, and social welfare work is about *encouraging participation* (see Boutellier & Boonstra, 2009). This lays the foundation for that communal narrative for administrators, citizens, and professionals which is so often absent (see Chapter 5).

Of course one can argue about the definitions of these core functions, but preferably not too much. The more difficult it is to achieve consensus about the substantive core practice (or the "attractor"), the more complicated it is for institutional representatives to have their say. The argument here is that the substantive core of public functions determines their design and that of the fields around them. Moreover, this identity defines its position in relation to other organizations. Improvisation presupposes a clear division of roles, but these will always be open to human interpretation, degrees of competence, and the formation of political blocs. This is why it is useful, even in a world without boundaries, to speak of a "society" – a geographically delineated whole of constituent parts, which in turn are also wholes. Their core functions guarantee their sustainability. This is getting close to a definition of public interest in the network society: its dynamic continuity.

The immanent meaning of practices

I have noted that society's common good can be thought of in terms of core functions of institutions. It is when these core functions are fixed that the organization's specific role becomes visible. This is something different from institutional interests, which are usually motivated by money. A credible contribution to the improvising society consists of process-oriented participation on the basis of substantive input. This last is what seems so difficult to imagine in practice (Tonkens et al., 2006b). Occasionally it seems as though professionals "forget" that their positions are based on (or should be based on) a meaning that inheres in the practice itself. The starting point for "a professional morality" is in the immanent meaning of social practices.

My ideas here are based on those of Alasdair MacIntyre, who defends and advocates for the quality inherent in human practices in his famous work *After virtue* (1981). A chess player strives to reach a higher level while operating within the rules of the game; this goal is inherent in the game, otherwise it makes no "sense." In other words, the good is already present to a certain degree from the moment that one engages in a certain practice. I discussed this idea in 1993 (reprinted in 2008, Chapter 7) and contrasted it to Richard Rorty's work (esp. 1989). MacIntyre argues fiercely in favor of reassessing virtue and invokes both classical and Christian traditions (Kinneging, 2005, was a similar undertaking).

Rorty is against every claim to moral truth, and thinks instead in terms of justification. Moral positions can at best prove their validity; this is why he calls himself a neo-pragmatist. His work is undoubtedly connected to the improvising society. His "post-modernist" vision is fully up-to-date, yet I arrive at a different opinion about MacIntyre's work when it comes to the meaning of practices for moral direction in a complex environment. Institutional practices form the basis of society, e.g., harmonization in structure, synchrony, and stability. The communal narrative is to be found in the practices.

Rorty (1986) points out in a footnote that MacIntyre's book has a peculiar caesura. The first part is a fierce attack on the emptiness of the emotionally governed morality ("emotivism") that remained after the Enlightenment. In the second part, however, he sketches an image of society that is built up out of practices in which individuals find coherence in what he calls "the narrative self." Individuals form their identities in institutional practices. This offers an important philosophical point of reference for public morality in the improvising society. The starting point is the inherent meaning of practices, with the understanding that we will always be inclined to argue about them.

The immanent meaning is not sacred, but often it stems from long traditions and historicity. Every practice, as it were, has developed its own canon. The WRR report on *Values, norms, and the burden of behavior* (*Waarden, normen en de last van gedrag,* 2004) viewed institutions as vehicles of public morality, but forgot to address the question of what they should be based on. For example, in certain middle schools educational goals have become secondary to maintaining order (Luiten, 2006, Chapter 3;

see also Boon, 2009). This is not a good situation. Rearing children in a family can lose its immanent meaning if the parents give way to their children's whims. "Household negotiating" finds its boundaries in the institution's core function. If there is a lack of shared "sense" in a practice, then it loses its meaning. Giving direction in practice begins with the practice itself, that is to say, the manner in which its core function has developed historically.

The immanent sense of purpose in such practices contains the possibility of bridging the gap between the solitary practice of the professional and the social mandate of his/her organization. Governance of social practices must be based on providing institutions with substantive mandates, which should fit well with professional practices. There should be agreement about the substantive core of the practice, otherwise it will be regarded as senseless. Education in numerous professions should be concerned with the core functions of their specific practices. Public morality depends on confident and self-aware institutions, whose social mandate might be more up for grabs than we tend to think.

The politics of improvising

Given society's institutional structure, which is based on its core functions, let me now return to the role of the government. Earlier I argued that the government's prominence in the ordering process should not be underestimated.[9] A meta-analysis of more than 800 scientific studies by Hill and Lynn (2005) also shows that hierarchical management by the government remains dominant: "the seemingly 'paradigmatic' shift away from hierarchical government toward horizontal governance (hence the increasing preference for 'governance' as an organizing concept) is less fundamental than it is tactical: new tools of administrative technologies are being added that facilitate public governance within a hierarchical system" (Hill & Lynn, 2005, p. 189).

According to these authors, the state retains its central position, even though there are now new techniques and new relations between different actors. The state is expanding its sphere of influence, but is also losing its grip. "The King is dead, long live the extended royal family" (Burris et al., 2008, p. 17). We are best served by a hybrid governmental position that begins by addressing how the social mandate of institutions is formulated and how their harmonization is organized.[10] Political interest centers on the clout of this extended family, and its democratic control. Networks can lack politically legitimated "meta-governance," as Sørenson called it (cited in Van Steden, 2010). This should relate both to new problems as well as new possibilities contained in the improvising society.

Problems and opportunities often have the same origin; my improvising society is concerned with three problem/opportunity dimensions. The first is *excluding* versus *opening* to other networks. We have seen from various perspectives that the network society creates a class of outsiders. Castells speaks of a "fourth world" of people who are not involved in the information society (2000b, pp. 70-165). Luhmann, whom we discussed earlier, also pointed out the danger of exclusion. This was in connection with the self-referential tendency of systems "to reconstruct external reality in conformity with the demands of internal coherence and cohesiveness" (cited by Burris et al., 2008, p. 28).

This is offset by the open character of the network society, which offers new possibilities for connecting and embracing other networks. The network society's lack of boundaries in principle offers continual opportunities for making new contacts and connections (social media).[11] We should also not underestimate the possibilities for the emergence of what have been called "lite" communities, for example, on the internet. At the same time, the improvising society does not mean the end of power relationships, inequality, and injustice, and can reproduce these in new forms.

The second problem/opportunity dimension is *hypercontrol* versus *diffusion* of power and opportunities. Various authors warn of a control society or the development of an authoritarian government. In previous chapters I described programs for achieving ordering. Without a doubt, these can take on more centralist and authoritarian features. On the other hand, permanent disruption is part of the improvising society's complexity. In a world without boundaries, central control seems by definition to be impossible. The problem, however, is that a hybrid government often cannot act with sufficient decisiveness.

This does not alter the fact that personal life is gradually being digitized. This kind of "control" is not so much the result of a totalitarian will to power (which has little chance in a complex democratic constitutional state) as the eager embrace of new technologies by administrators and citizens, either out of convenience or urgency. This same kind of mechanism was described by Robert Reich (2007) in the rise of super capitalism. Reich attributes this to the conflation of roles as citizen, employee, consumer, and investor (e.g., in a pension fund), which makes opposition impossible. In an information state the roles of citizen, consumer, potential victim, and potential criminal all come together. This is Foucault's dreaded culmination of the micro-physics of power (1977).[12]

The third problem/opportunity dimension concerns the *fear of chaos vs. trust in ordering*. I have tried to defuse this fear by pointing out the ordering processes that are at work, always and everywhere. As I have stated before, networks are not the source but the solution to complexity, even though they create a great deal of fuss and confusion. I specifically addressed the ambiguity in the emergence of order with the concept of improvisation. Processes of organization and disruption are continually on the agenda, and preferably lead (even if only temporarily) to fine-tuning processes that result in harmony, the feeling that it is "all right." This popular term is a totally inadequate concept, yet I find it appropriate for describing how the fine-tuning of actors gives direction and create momentum. I emphasize the importance of normative direction here.

The opportunities side of the improvising society presupposes a political strategy. The network society apparently suffers from a lack of security and reassurance, which should be resolved from the perspective of a dynamic social continuity. On the other hand, the improvising society offers possibilities for experimentation, innovation, and vitality in local, small-scale settings around concrete problems, ideas, and/or ideals (Burris et al., 2008).[13] The realization that the improvising society makes forms of "micro-governance" possible, above and beyond major organizations and massive structures, is challenging to say the least. These conditions make it possible to find a middle way between deafening cacophony and moments of scintillating harmony.

CONCLUDING REMARKS

THE DYNAMICS OF ORGANIZED FREEDOM

This volume examines social order; the conclusion is that we live in an improvising society. Improvisational music such as jazz is thus a fitting metaphor for the current social order. This is not just a clever comparison, but one based on empirical and theoretical grounds, which I did explain. Having this characterisation with its associated diagnosis does not really solve any problems, but it does create an opening to a new era, an era in which it is no longer necessary to look continuously to the past. We have become too attached to the image of society as one enormous system of values and norms, a world of common citizenship under an overarching order. This blinkers our ability to see the possibilities and outcomes hidden in our immediate environment, both physical and virtual.

Small worlds in a big society

One of the most troublesome problems in this study was keeping the themes of order, public morality, and authority stable, without losing sight of just how fragmented the reality is. For many years various authors have predicted the end of everything – equality, justice, public morality, and respect for the state. These very topics have always been of great concern to me because of my aversion to cruelty, moral decline, and coarse behavior. This is why I oppose a "let it all hang out" approach to scholarship and gratuitous revelations. In this work I search for a representation of social order that makes problems manageable and promotes good quality of life.

I am also aware of the risks involved in this enterprise. The desire for "the good life" can have unpleasant consequences.

Systems of control, inspections, regulators, and monitors are increasingly prevalent, as is a strong tendency toward discipline and repressive policies. There is a cry for great leaders and great narratives. The aversion to disorder can be so powerful that the opposite – a culture of control – is achieved. It is against this backdrop that I discussed, in the second part of this book, three programs for social order – civilization, security, and citizenship – that strive to systematically reduce the complexity of society. They are used with varying degrees of success, and they teach us about people's need for social order, especially when that order is not so easily achieved.

Between the two extremes of laissez-faire policies and excessive control, I observe that there is more social order than we seem to think. It is not "over" us, however, but "around" us. This is the broader notion of many small worlds[1] that I explored in this book. The network society – the core concept of this volume – is still based on the institutions that give a modern society its stability: the government in all her capacities and layers; the legal system with its finely-tuned forms, protocols, and checks and balances; and also health care, education, and housing corporations – the institutions of the European welfare state. Together they form the twentieth century's material realization of the common good. And then there are the market forces – the globalizing business community based on profit-seeking and self-interest that is a condition for welfare – and the organizations of civil society (family, church, and social).

The triangle of state, market, and society is constantly seeking equilibrium. Currently there is talk of a shift from the state to the community, where blind faith in market forces has also shrunk. In the UK there is talk of the "big society," a concept that is also increasingly popular in the Netherlands (see Blond 2010 for an interesting analysis). After the neoliberalism of Margaret Thatcher and the authoritarian, welfare state socialism of Tony Blair,[2] there is now a clear trend toward *social responsibility*. The various organizations of state, market, and society offer stability – this is nothing new – but the forms in which that happens are under pressure and are behaving differently.

Jazzy structures

The social institutions are still standing, but they must move with the times. Society no longer shapes itself around institutions; rather, the institutions must fold themselves around the events in an impulsive and fragmented society. They must adjust to what I call "complexity without direction" in Part One. There is much administrative busyness, complex cooperative relationships, and competition, yet precious few communal ideals, shared norms, and agreed-upon courses of action. This leads to feelings of being adrift, insecure, and orphaned. Our current society is not easily captured in a few brush strokes. Of course that was never the case, but the current fragmentation sharpens the contrast, as does the corresponding appeal for its repair. Yet it is this very concept of "one whole" – a single entity – that severely hinders us.

Our national societies are single entities to a certain extent, but they are not "all of a piece." They are made up of many entities, which in turn can be parts of other entities. And so the whole of society is composed of various wholes, which also contain other parts and wholes. This is an unbounded and fragmented order. Jazzy structures can be difficult to grasp, given their myriad variations, but they are not lacking in organization and continuity. The concept of an "improvising society" offers a glimmer of hope while also hinting at an implied criticism. Call it "positive cultural criticism." In the improvising society, one often has to row with whatever oars are available, to use a Dutch expression. Improvisation can even be an excuse for just messing around: "Oh, well. We live in a wing-it-as-you-go society anyway." A clear narrative is missing, and this can make us indifferent to everything and everybody. Who cares?

From that perspective, an improvising society can evoke frightening images of "every man for himself," with winners and losers. A great deal of tinkering and muddling goes on with child protective services, nursing homes, police departments, politics, educational institutions, and government departments and ministries, not to mention the business community, the retailers, and the self-employed. All this hubbub within the triangle of government, market, and society creates the image of an improvising society. Given its conflicts, contradictions, and major problems, there is plenty to criticize. And yet I regard it as an image of organized freedom in jazzy structures, and especially one with the potential for order. When successful, it is perhaps the highest degree of human organization possible.

The art of improvisation

Improvisation always happens within a certain context. I am thinking specifically of music, but this is true for other artistic expressions and spontaneous behaviors in general. Even a soloist without accompanying musicians plays within the environment in which he finds himself, the musical lineage to which he belongs and the education he received, and for an audience that is willing to listen. Improvisation cannot exist outside of context, and the same is true for other forms of music or art, or culture in general. Spontaneity and creative freedom are distinguishing characteristics of improvisation, yet at the same time improvisation is bound by the principles within which it occurs. Attempts to break free from all conventions or agreements are illusory. Experimental or free jazz is almost impossible to listen to – unless the musician is a consummate master of his/her instrument and also follows at least some musical convention (often provocatively, even defiantly). The music can be completely experimental, but not completely chaotic. By definition the musician is bound by what music sounded like in the past.

Improvised music is both freedom and organization, an analogy that also fits contemporary social order. Let us look at several ideal-typical characteristics. The improvising society gives individuals the room to excel, and that space is intentionally created and given by others who are supportive at that point in time. This collaboration involves fine-tuning through feedback mechanisms, which are usually based on agreed-upon themes, repeating motifs, and general principles. One needs to know what one is about. Trust and reciprocity are involved. If the investment is large, or the result unpredictable, then the need for control increases. The individual space then shrinks. There are good reasons for this, but a society that functions on a basis of distrust and control is not functional. It is also not habitable; it is a totalitarian state.

An important characteristic of the improvising society is the assignment of roles. Just as the pianist is not expected to play the trumpet, social actors must know who they are and what others expect of them. Cooperation is hopeless if everyone tries to do the same thing. There must be a collective goal, but resources are not equally spread around. A productive collaboration is based on uniquely individual inputs, and those inputs should be positive. The participants must have something to offer: knowledge and experience, skills and ideas, ideals and opinions. Ideally, this characteristic keeps the improvising society from shifting into an "anything goes" mode, which can happen on occasion. Role and capability come together to form what might be called identity, the idea of the uniqueness or singular nature or being of an individual (person, organization, society). The network society does not limit the formation of identity, but rather enhances it. Indeed, social media revolve around identity formation.

Introducing spontaneity to a structure at just the right moment; identity in relation to tradition, knowledge, and skills in order to excel; and a motif or theme that resonates and thus creates a sense of community – these are all characteristics of the improvising society. There is one more characteristic that springs to mind. I call it leadership lite, as practiced by the lead player who sets the tone, harmony, and direction for the band. That is a different kind of leadership from the ideologically inspired type that led the masses to the Promised Land in the twentieth century. Although the yearning for such a leader still exists (media logic demands vigor, for example), the practice of public management is different. Leadership has not gone away but has simply been scattered about, to be picked up and pocketed by a variety of more or less appealing figures.

Organic intellectuals

Individuals or organizations willing to take the lead are required in order to get things moving. At present there are many candidates available, although well-defined leadership positions are usually not widely available. This results in a great deal of arguing over competence and questions about control, management, governance, and leadership. Especially in management circles, "leadership" is a "big deal." Much is expected in the way of inspiring leadership, yet most people have difficulty with someone who claims to lead them, unless he or she is their own chosen guru. The network society does have leadership figures, but nobody is inclined to listen to them. This is the tragedy of modern politicians; it is not clear whom they represent. There is a peculiar yearning for leadership, yet no one is allowed to lead.

Leadership in the improvising society is essentially something different. It is about laying down themes, making agreements, connecting within or among networks, offering room to excel, and organizing collaboration. It is about "leadership lite," which can still entail heavy work before being achieved. In general, the boss is not someone who demands, but one who oversees and supports the process without trying to avoid final responsibility. Leadership should be earned, and that applies to every authority not attached to a previously defined position of power (see Chapter 7). Authority today arises where it shows itself to be relevant. Even police officers do not have self-evident authority, even though they may have power. That applies equally to teachers, parents, employers, and leaders.

These personas or actors have a slight advantage in that they are vested with some institutional authority. However, if they do not perform well, such authority is almost useless. Authority in the improvising society means granting credibility and meaningful significance to routines and protocols, social relationships and possibilities, and solutions. Instead of a vertical hierarchy of authority, our culture has a diversified authority structure that is embedded within a maze of networks, clusters, circuits, and social connections. This is why I regard the Italian

Marxist Antonio Gramsci's concept of "organic intellectuals" (1971) as applicable and useful.[3] In the 1930s Gramsci concerned himself (partly while in prison) with the role of intellectuals in class struggle. Gramsci was of the opinion that every individual is an intellectual because of his or her rational capabilities, but not every individual can realize that potential. There is a secondary, derivative role. According to Gramsci, these persons are not an isolated elite but rather the people involved in the routine practices and protocols of organizations. They are not researchers but rather organic intellectuals who give meaning to the experiences and feelings of the group they represent. Their function is recognizable in the "leadership lite" of the improvising society.

Gramsci hoped that the organic intellectuals of the working class would eventually mobilize their intellectual capability and create a bond between daily *praxis* and historical potential. Today this goal can be legitimately rejected as megalomaniac and inherently totalitarian. It represents a current of thought that made the twentieth century violent (a topic that is too large to discuss here). However, in the network society, Gramsci's organic intellectualism is relevant as a marker of diversified authority – leadership lite – that gives credible meaning to network communities. In other words, organic intellectualism that is not connected with a larger movement or historical necessity, as Gramsci surmised, but in relation to other networks that in turn also generate organic intellectualism.

Meritocracy and improvisation

To my mind, this interpretation of leadership offers the opportunity to think in terms of forming an elite, while at the same time avoiding the idea of an aristocratic elite. That kind of elite has lost much of its social significance, having (among other things) shaken off its classic responsibility (Ossenwaarde, 2007). The new elite is diverse and dispersed among organizations, networks, and practices which together give the improvising society meaning, and therefore direction. Its members are not always equally successful; they are often overpaid, but less inarticulate than we think. The process of giving meaning is also dispersed, but not chaotic. This form of leadership is less megalomaniacal, less heroic, and less authoritarian than was thought possible historically, yet it is crucial for the quality of society.

The growth of a diverse elite brings with it a new tragedy, one predicted years ago by Michael Young (1958). After social equality has been achieved, variation in levels and types of education (based on individual talents and social possibilities) becomes a determining factor. Such variation sharpens the contrast between success and failure, the capable people and the underachievers, and higher and lower educational degrees. Bovens and Wille (2010) set out to show how education makes a difference in the matter of class distinctions, and how this creates new lines of inequality and thus a breeding ground for frustration and resentment.

Participating in an improvising society requires a variety of skills. Besides being able to maintain identity (role and capability), people must also be able to interact with others – they must have networking skills, as it is called in employment ads, both physical and digital. And then one needs to understand how individual skills and networks relate to other sets of skills and networks. That is asking a lot, and not everyone is capable of this. Inclusiveness – ensuring that everyone can take part – is one of the biggest challenges of the network society. However, I consider the model of a new two-class society too schematic to fully fathom the question of in-groups and out-groups.

The network society is too fragmented to think in terms of two segments. Class differences are dissolved or atomized into a much subtler cloud of connections, contacts, possibilities, problems, and opportunities. A two-class society is too monolithic and also rather denigrating for those who have a lower level of education. Schooling increases opportunities, but less education does not mean a person has no chances. On the contrary, there are many ways to find one's path through the labyrinth of networking possibilities. Organizing one's life and its personal networks is not reserved only for the highly educated.

In a world without borders, the "cosmopolitan class" is well off, even though it is not hegemonic, or powerful in the traditional sense. Even more to the point, there are legitimate complaints about today's transient, even nomadic "hordes." This may well be cause for concern, but it also shows that the less educated are not just oppressed and invisible. In fact, a network society that is inclusive is a good starting point for a political program.

Social continuity

This new conclusion to the second Dutch edition gives an overview of a number of the arguments in this study. The tone and style are different from the main text, which is based on scholarly and scientific literature. Despite its academic character, this book seems to appeal to those whom I regard as organic intellectuals: the professionals, managers, directors, and policy makers who are responsible for church organizations or schools, housing authorities or positions in civil service. These persons know they are involved in the community, yet they often experience feelings of helplessness. "What is my role in the greater scheme of things?" Complexity without direction paralyzes if we don't understand that our energies cannot be derived from grand narratives and ideals, impassioned leaders and ideologists, solid structures and eternal virtues. We cannot find social order at the front, leading the way; rather it is to be found within routines, work patterns, and experience. Social order develops within this multitude of activities, thus giving continuity to the community.

That is also the answer to the normative contradiction that we must have something "in common." A complex world cannot be steered by grand ideas or great narratives, but it does recognize social continuity. Social order is based on the assumption that we – people, organizations, communities – will continue in some form or another. That is quite a simple but fundamental idea. It is also why "sustainability" is such an attractive political notion. It addresses not only the environment, but also physical, social, and economic systems and processes. Sustainability can be understood as responsible continuity, or conservation.

How people contribute to that in a world without boundaries is a question of personal insights, debates regarding those issues, and (if necessary) social conflict. This is where, in principle, the improvisations come together. How do my efforts relate to those of others, with an eye to the continuity of our community? Perhaps not much, but neither are they nothing.

EPILOGUE

We have been searching for the patterns that give direction to society. Because these are increasingly difficult to discern, I have examined specific ordering processes and borrowed from the vocabularies of other scholarly domains in order to make these societal developments more visible, and hence more open to discussion. This is the minimum requirement for any discussion of their truth. I set out these processes once again below, and reflect on their psychological consequences – how reassuring can a world of improvisations be? I then give a brief scholarly justification for my findings.

The term "improvising society" contains numerous meanings. There is the suggestion of helping out, rowing with the oars we have. New conditions compel us to action, first-aid fixes, and managerial pressure; to an ad-hoc policy, fumbling around, experimenting, and overly hasty legislation. In that sense, improvisation is synonymous with makeshift, temporary, and working with whatever is available. It refers to the impotence I discussed at the beginning of this book, which causes us to experience life as mainly chaotic. Having now come to the end of my book, I hope I have made it clear that improvisation can offer us a perspective. Indeed, I find it useful to regard improvisation as a metaphor for the social ordering of the boundless world. It is the human variant of complexity in nature.

Second, the improvising society also refers to new social forms, which at their core are about fine-tuning. In both tightly structured and more fluid compositions, arrangements and spontaneous play produce a kaleidoscopic image of networks, clusters, and subcultures. The relations between the constituent identities can be laid down in the form of written agreements about motifs, themes (possibly in contract form), and perspectives (problem definitions and analyses), or are based on the intent to respond reciprocally to one another.

Third, the improvising society reflects new institutional relations. Institutions develop on the basis of tradition and renewal, and give society stability. The core functions of institutions and organizations – identities – provide the center of gravity for coherence and cooperation. The legal system has a unique position here, but other institutions are also carriers of self-evident social continuity. Law, informal regulation, and self-evidence give normative direction. This book aims also to give an image of this third societal meaning, in which the first two are implied.

The improvising society enjoys – ideally speaking – freedom from role stability in the fine-tuning and agreed-upon patterns. This sometimes leads to success, but is also often forced or doomed to failure. Social ordering based on internalized inequality is resolved through ordering on the basis of synchronization among individuals, roles, and functions. The fine-tuning of one actor (person, organization) with another actor, and vice versa, *ad infinitum,* is the ordering process of the current network society. It comes about ad hoc, finds its place self-evidently, or is regulated by one means or another. In the last case, the normative setting determines the amount of governance from above. The improvising society is governed in a hybrid combination of functional authority and synchronous movement

I regard improvisation as a metaphor, but one with a high degree of reality. It determines the social staging of the network society, both in a structural and a moral sense. Structurally, improvisation is the answer to the complexity I discussed – the constituting elements form assemblages amid many other assemblages. The concept of assemblage comes from the French philosopher Gilles Deleuze. There are countless relations between the positions taken in this work and his philosophy.[1] I chose not to make this relation explicit, because his work has already been well discussed by others.

Improvisation also gives moral direction. In the search for coherent interplay, participants need identity, and in turn they explore the reliability of other identities. This exploration can be based on the historical core functions of institutions and the manner in which they translate into a social contract. It is in the totality of all these fine-tunings that a society is "expressed." Its identity is built up from other identities, and the task of politics is to articulate this in a convincing manner – giving credible significance to wholes that are based on other wholes.

What, for example, is "the Netherlands," with her diverse communities, her history of cast-off social pillars, and her jaded prosperity – or whatever other ingredients a politician may use to spin a convincing narrative? Cultural ambivalence (illustrated in the Introduction by the reactions to Geert Wilders' anti-Muslim propaganda video *Fitna*) points to the fundamental ambiguity of the improvising society, an ambiguity that is abiding. That may be a consolation, and it might even offer hope (e.g., Braithwaite, 2004). That hope can be borrowed from the fundamental boundlessness of the world, the rediscovery of one's individual surroundings, the limited range of one's actions, and organizations that are independent yet at the same time related to others.

This statement of hope brings me to the outer perimeter of the domain of the sciences, although some may think that I transgressed it much earlier. The current study can be regarded as a form of interpretive social science. There are three problems with this approach. First there is the risk of irresponsible speculation and overgeneralization. No hard empirical evidence can be found for many of the statements in this book – not because it does not exist, but because it *cannot* exist. The concept of the improvising society, for example, has no material substrate; at best this can be found in empirical references, for example, in the documented problems of administrators and professionals. In such a case, the burden of proof lies not in empirical correspondence, but in the coherence of individual reasoning of those involved (see Walker, 1989). This book steers between correspondence and coherence, hoping to convince rather than to prove.

A second problem is the interdisciplinary nature of this endeavor. I have drawn freely from all possible (academic) sources and assembled my own product from them. My book

The safety utopia was regarded by some as idiosyncratic (De Haan, 2003). I regarded that as a compliment, because it is precisely at the borders between disciplines that a conceptual dynamic arises. Kodwo Eshun (1998, 186) talks about this in terms of "concept engineering: using different concepts to probe new areas of experience, to anticipate and fastforward different explorations into new fields of perception which are always there but whose strength lies in that they don't exist in traditional mainstream terms."

The third problem with this study is its normative character. Occasionally, when certain situations are reviewed, normative pronouncements pop up in the descriptive analyses. I regard the improvising society not only as an adequate interpretation, but also as a meaningful policy-administrative description that I hope others find useful. In this sense, a more philosophical ambition of determination or justification also plays a role. Michael Power (2007) calls this "fitting theory": "The method is one of progressively and continuously refashioning a family of arguments in a process of self-critical writing, a constant and restless trade and exchange between theoretical precepts and bits of the empirical world, each mutually explicating the other in a 'to and fro' process as Habermas once put it (*hin- und hergerissen*)" (p. ix).

Using a similar approach means that I give absolute short shrift to the careful research done in the disciplines I have used. I apologize in advance to all the scholarly colleagues who think I have unjustifiably ignored their insights. My own work is more about the broad perspective than the details. There is a cartoon called "The World of Science" in which dozens of tiny figures are digging holes so deep that they can no longer see each other. I think a helicopter ride over this world of learning is useful in order to discover the coherent patterns. I realize that I have been overly ambitious, and perhaps irresponsibly so. In a real sense, *The improvising society* is itself a typical product of a boundless world.

NOTES

Chapter 1

1 As early as 1959, an article in *Public Administration Review* described "muddling through" as the only managerial option (Lindblom 1959).

2 And this against a backdrop of agents and organizations such as *Beroeps(z)eer* [Professional honor/pain] and the *Vereniging voor Beter Onderwijs* [Association for Better Education]. See Noordegraaf (2004) for a serious defense of the new management.

3 See Wrong (1995) for an interesting overview.

4 From community (*Gemeinschaft*) to society (*Gesellschaft*) (Tönnies in 1887), from mechanical to organic solidarity (Durkheim in 1893), and from a sacred to a profane order (Becker and Barnes in 1961) – as described by Sztompka (2002).

5 The reverse – the moral design of social space – can be defended, but I deliberately give public morality primacy (Boutellier, 2002, pp. 42f.). The design in relation to morality and behavior points to a fundamental debate (see Chapter 3).

6 To avoid any misunderstanding: for many, God and community continue to be sources of direction, although collectively they have lost their self-evident authority. We tend to think principally in terms of diversification and self-determination (Taylor, 2007).

7 Published in English as *Crime and Morality* (Boutellier, 2000).

8 Not incidentally, at the same time as the secularization process.

9 Despite this success, in 2006 Jan van Dijk (see also 2008a) argued in an inaugural speech for recognition of the victim. For a review, see Boutellier (2007a).

10 Published in English as *The Safety Utopia* (Boutellier, 2004).

11 I use the word "pattern" here somewhat casually, although it takes on a deeper meaning in Pieters' "pattern-oriented approach to complexity" (2010).

12 With the caveat that most victims of political Muslim terrorist activities are in Muslim nations.

13 A combination of "agitation" and "propaganda," and originally used in communist circles.

14 A theme that Giddens developed with Beck and Lash (1994).

15 *Sociaal en Cultureel Planbureau* [The Netherlands Institute for Social Research], in *Continu Onderzoek Burgerperspectieven*; Dekker & Steenvoorden (2008).

16 The current interest in the art of living is set against this backdrop; see, e.g., Dohmen (2007).

17 The Dutch report also laconically mentions multiple identities. Radicalized youth, for example, have trouble combining a variety of identities (Gielen, 2008).

18 The bureaucratic criteria par excellence for giving form to the substantive normativity of politics (Weber, 1947)
19 A reference to the pragmatic "What works?" that has become so popular in the Dutch social domain (e.g., Mak et al., 2010). I regard this as a meaningful approach, which fits the current conditions (see, e.g., Boutellier et al., 2008), but it is not the topic of this book.
20 The Austrian-born philosopher Sir Karl Popper spoke of "piecemeal engineering," comparable to the narrow margins of democracy to which Joop den Uyl, former leader of the Dutch Labor Party (PvdA), referred.
21 The "frame" concept comes from Ervin Goffman, who described its various effects (1974). This concept is now commonplace in the new social sciences dealing with management, organization, and communications.
22 Benin guitarist Lionel Loneke characterized jazz improvisation as "organized freedom" (*De Groene Amsterdammer*, 27 June 2008, p. 34). That remark ultimately inspired the title of this book. The analogy with jazz improvisation, however, is not mine originally (for example Dohman, 2008).

Chapter 2

1 See Boutellier (2004, Chapter 2) for a discussion of Beck.
2 The American-Dutch historian James Kennedy (1995) described a similar Dutch radicalism in the 1960s, which came into existence through the relatively easy change of course by the authorities.
3 He wrote five books on this concept within a very short period; it can be said that there is a lot of overlap.
4 This theme is familiar from Erich Fromm, *Escape from freedom* (1941).
5 Bauman (2000, p. 2) refers to the Communist Manifesto by Engels and Marx, who wrote about "melting the solids," so that new solids could form.
6 The waste management industry holds a prominent place in "liquid life's economy" – creative destruction (Bauman, 2005, p. 3).
7 In this context, privacy is experienced completely differently. What once was private has become public, both in the area of security (cameras, preventive body searches, etc.) and in personal experience (intimate phone calls in a crowded train, internet exposure, and the like). This explains why the protection of privacy has become a somewhat unpopular form of engagement.
8 Bauman borrows from René Girard the insight that communities need victims – outsiders – who serve to mark the boundaries (but they should be not too far from the community) (2000, p. 194).
9 In my opinion, the Dutch concept of security, which I characterized earlier as a semantic dragnet (2005), is gaining the same status.
10 For an elaboration of gated communities as the future, see Boutellier et al. (2005).

11 In this context the cultural-anthropological concept "liminal zone," which refers to the twilight area between the normal world and ecstasy, is relevant (Hobbs et al., 2002).
12 A comparable ethnographic study was published in the Netherlands by De Jong (2007). He emphasized the group psychological processes of street culture.
13 The authors were strongly influenced by Lacanian psychoanalysis, in which a distinction is made between imaginary identification (convergence with one's own primal desires) and symbolic identification (the striving for a higher "ideal"). Lacan also distinguishes the "real," or internal reality (for an introduction to the work of Lacan, see Zizek, 2007).
14 Consumerism, "the desire and ability to consume at a level far above basic needs," goes back to the eighteenth century (Veblen, cited by Hall et al., 2008, p. 89).
15 Dalrymple's (2001) commentary on leftist intelligentsia is recognizable here. It does not lay out the relation to neoliberalism in the 1990s.
16 A similar discussion took place in the Netherlands in the 1970s, when e.g. the criminologist Jongman viewed criminality as a form of resistance (for a review, see Boutellier, 2000, Chapter 2).
17 Later in this chapter we will examine the views of the German philosopher Peter Sloterdijk regarding this same motivation, which he thinks has no outlet in the current era.
18 Sloterdijk endorses Fukuyama's (1992) famous thesis that, after the victory of political liberalism, no further alternatives are available, which is different than that there will be no further conflicts.
19 Resentment refers to the psychology of victimhood and as such is "the most shared article in the world" (p. 63). Often victims cannot and will not forgive and forget. They prefer to amplify the pain rather than making it more bearable: "lifting themselves out of the depression of suffering through the elation of misery" (p. 64).
20 The following conclusions can be drawn, based on population surveys (Vollaard et al., 2009). There has been a decline in crime since the mid 1990s (and by at least 25 percent between 2002 and 2008). This is mainly due to a decline in the number of thefts, which increased in 1992. Violence and vandalism declined steeply after 2003, but this decline did not last. Around 2002 there was also a small wave of increased victimhood. Differences between areas and regions need to be accounted for.
21 This was in response to the international emails received about an artist's project; she had turned her dead cat into a handbag, "a cat bag."

Chapter 3

1 For example, Van Agt (the ethical revival) and Hirsch Ballin (1994).
2 In the *Volkskrant*, Forum page (June 25, 2007).
3 In all immodesty, I believe I contributed to this discussion. Witness the qualification "moral crusader" that Daems (2008, Chapter 4) applied to me in his dissertation.
4 The LPF (Pim Fortuyn List) was the protest party that remained after the upcoming politician was assassinated on May 6, 2002.
5 To the best of my knowledge there is no report of this meeting available. Journalist Martin Sommer drew the same conclusion in the *Volkskrant* (June 25, 2004, p. 27).
6 Van den Brink (2004b) elaborated this idea further.
7 *Moderniteit als opgave* (2007) is a good overview of Van den Brink's work that unfortunately has not received sufficient attention.
8 Which does not reflect how urgent the question of security was in 2002, the year of Fortuyn's assassination, or at least how urgent security was perceived to be at that time. The crisis of political legitimacy should be guaranteed by the central pillar supporting the legitimacy of national authority – *securitas*.
9 The first sentence in Dalrymple's *Life at the bottom* is a glitzy reference to *Marx's Communist Manifesto*: "A specter is haunting the Western world: the underclass" (2001, p. vii). The Dutch translation was published in 2004.
10 Dalrymple's ascent with the Dutch-speaking public began with his (at the time very conservative) supplement *Letter & geest* [Letter & spirit] in the daily newspaper *Trouw*.
11 In the relevant chapter, "The uses of corruption," Dalrymple comes to a surprisingly positive review of Italian circumstances.
12 This is apparent, for example, in the debate over integration, in which conservatism was sentenced to defend the free world, while categorically rejecting its decadent manifestations.
13 At that time Spruyt was director of the Edmund Burke Foundation in the Netherlands.
14 To this end, I use Spruyt's previously cited book, as well as an article from Kinneging (2000, also 2005, chapter 24). I also use Baudet and Visser (2010).
15 In 2004 Spruyt wanted to collaborate with the populist politician Geert Wilders, which alienated his sympathizers.
16 This idea resulted in Kinneging's *The geography of good and evil* (2011; original Dutch 2005), a voluminous treatise on individual, familial, and public virtues. His earlier thesis (1997; original Dutch 1995) dealt with the relationship between the aristocracy and the classics.
17 The book was published in the UK under the title *What's the matter with America?*
18 Ultimately the conservatives did not achieve any of the items on their agenda. In 2009 Frank gave a merciless critique of the eight

years of George W. Bush's administration titled *The wrecking crew: How conservatives ruined government, enriched themselves, and beggared the nation.*

19 See, for example, Bartels (2006).

20 Smith devoted an interesting chapter to the importance of rhetoric in the sense of priorities, frames, and positions taken (Smith, 2007, Chapter 2).

21 Preceded by a crime policy that was shaped in the mid-1980s by the government's announced policy *Samenleving en criminaliteit* [Society and crime] (1985).

Chapter 4

1 As opposed to physical safety (disasters and crisis situations).

2 I have been concerned with this issue almost all of my professional life (e.g., Boutellier, 1993 [2008], 2002, 2005, 2007b). For a descriptive review of my work, see Daems (2008, Chapter 4). In this chapter I focus on the shifts in meaning, from the idea that concepts give to practices meaning and drives them further.

3 Krol has also voiced his opinion of the Dutch penal system in essay form. See *Voor wie kwaad wil* [For those who want to harm] (1990), and also Krol (1998).

4 This was the title of the abridged trade edition of Hermann Franke's dissertation in 1996.

5 Norbert Elias's theory of the civilizing process found support among sociologists in Amsterdam (especially De Swaan, e.g. his inaugural speech in 1979).

6 Franke's work covers the period up to the end of the 1980s.

7 The actual capacity of the prison population in the Netherlands grew in the period from 1990 to 2007 from 7,677 to 18,919; in 2008 this dropped somewhat to 17,070 (Leertouwer & Kalidien, 2009, p. 533).

8 For a precise teasing apart of the governance theory behind the white paper, see Van Noije and Wittebrood (2008).

9 I described these bridges earlier in *Meer dan veilig* [More than secure] (2005). Here I discuss their consequences.

10 The WRR expressly argued for a preventive approach (2008) in the case of physical forms of safety.

11 The French criminologist Wacquant is of the opinion that a comparatively similar punitive development is taking place in Europe as in the United States. For a review of the work of this "activist criminologist," see Daems (2008, Chapter 5).

12 This quartering (Boutellier, 2005) was recently tested using Q methodology, which showed that the experience does have indeed four different factors (Spithoven, 2010).

13 See www.cbs.nl/nl-NL/menu/themas/veiligheid-recht/publicaties/artikelen/archief/2010/2010-3024-wm.htm.

14 It is interesting to note the title of a strategic report from the Ministry of Justice: *Justice = social cohesion* (2009a).

15 I reached a similar finding in research on nuisance behavior in the 1990s titled "systematic intimidation" (Boutellier & Vinke, 2002).
16 Personal communication, October 2009.
17 Incidentally, a revision to the ASBO policy was announced at the end of 2010.
18 Van Kempen (2008) points to a shift in the rights of the individual in a judgment by the European Court of Human Rights (Osman vs. United Kingdom, 1998), in which a positive obligation is ascribed to the government to protect the lives of citizens threatened by third parties.
19 In the Netherlands, banning persons caught shoplifting from entering shops (Schuilenburg & Van Calster, 2009).
20 Risks are also necessary for a vibrant civil society; they create opportunities and are a basic premise of the free enterprise system (O'Malley, 2004, Chapter 3).
21 Recently it seemed to me that a group of law students understood the concept of legal protection as protection from other citizens, which lends anecdotal support to my description of the shift in meaning.
22 An important theme in my research program Security & Citizenship at the VU University of Amsterdam (see, e.g., Hageman, 2008; Boutellier & De Groot, 2010; Broekhuizen, 2010).

Chapter 5

1 Prime Minister Lubbers' remark in 1990 that the Netherlands "is sick" can be regarded as the political turning point in appraisal of the citizen. That now seems outdated; the Netherlands today is primarily angry.
2 Van Gunsteren (1998), the authority on this subject, distinguishes between, for example, libertarian, communitarian, and neo-republican citizenship.
3 Besides the question of dual passports, there is the problem of the illegal stateless, or "denizens" (Shearing & Wood, 2003).
4 He expands further on the classifications of Terpstra and Kouwenhoven (2004) and Kroes (2006).
5 For example, the Neighborhood Secure (*Buurt Veilig*) project in Deventer, in which citizens help decide when to deploy the police. Amsterdam has a similar project, My Neighborhood Better (*Mijn Buurt Beter*). The principle was borrowed from British Reassurance Policing, in which citizens are systematically asked about "signal crimes," which are then given priority (see Innes, 2004).
6 See Low (2003). In the Netherlands gated communities are not common (see Scholte, 2008) and are mainly limited to settlements for seniors.
7 Paul Scheffer (2007) regards this as the core of the relationship between established residents and newcomers in a new homeland.
8 The "preferred term" introduced by Minister Van der Laan in his brief on integration to the Dutch Parliament (*Tweede Kamer*) (2009).

9 As argued in detail in the WRR report on the Dutch identity (2007).
10 This is why I have argued for a preamble to the Dutch Constitution that specifically protects pluralism (Boutellier, 2008a).

Chapter 6

1 The brief lifecycle of concepts is a hallmark of the information era. The euphoria surrounding "the network society" has subsided, but the concept's relevance, in my opinion, is still immense.
2 The word "nodal" comes from the Latin *nodus*: 'knot,' or connection point.
3 Castells speaks of a third revolution, after the first two Industrial Revolutions – from 1770-1800 (the steam engine) and from 1870-1900 (electricity). The third technological revolution started in 1970 (the transistor). The first two revolutions produced cheap new sources of energy. The third brought a new resource – information.
4 Approximately 25 percent of children in the United States do not live with two parents; 50 percent do not live with their biological parents (Castells, 2004, p. 196f.).
5 Richard Sennett (1998) published a comparative analysis of the undermining power of flexible labor.
6 Castells (2004) analyses four socially "fundamental" grassroots movements – the Mexican Zapatistas, the American patriotic movement, the Japanese Aum Shinrykio, and the Arabic Al Qaeda. He also examines anti-globalists, the green movement, and feminism (in relation to the end of the patriarchal family), in which new identities are sought.
7 Van den Brink (2006) detected too little order in the public space and too much in social institutions; both stem from the same cause.
8 Castells (2004, p. 402f.) is of the opinion that corruption is not really increasing, but confidence in politics is waning. On integrity and related policy, see Huberts (2005) and Huberts et al. (2008).
9 A Canadian sociologist of Dutch origin, and (on a personal note) the spouse of Richard Sennett.
10 An English translation was published in 1996; I refer to the revised version published in 2006.
11 Forerunners of the idea that society should be understood as a network were Craven and Wellman (1973), Martin (1978), and Hiltz and Turoff (1978). All these authors started from the perspective of developing media; Hiltz and Turoff included the computer. To Craven and Wellman falls the honor of being the first to ask the "community question" in 1973: Should we regard the urban society as a community, or is it more like a totality of networks?
12 Data need meaning to become information (Pieters, 2010).
13 Taylor wrote *The principles of scientific management* (1911), in which he argued for rationalizing labor. The assembly line in Ford factories (introduced in 1913) is regarded as the prototypical example.
14 A concept taken from the German philosopher Jürgen Habermas.

15 The theme of *Omstreden ruimte* [Contested space] (Boutellier et al., 2009a).
16 For example, the relationship between "street coaches" in Amsterdam (Van Steden & Jones, 2008) and social workers (both professionals) who visit the homes of hooligans.
17 In this connection see Katz and Rice (2002).
18 A concept introduced by the French sociologist Pierre Bourdieu (1986), which has since entered the standard sociological vocabulary.
19 Van Dijk wrote about this in *The deepening divide* (2005).
20 A Sunday edition of the *New York Times* apparently contains more information than a cultivated *burger* of the seventeenth century encountered in his entire life.
21 Management studies in particular seem to contain an abundance of twaddle inspired by chaos theory.
22 *Complexus* is Latin for tissue, fabric, web.
23 I am grateful to Kees Pieters for his comments on this chapter.
24 This paragraph is based on network specialist Albert-László Barabási's book, *Linked* (2002).
25 Research by Stanley Milgram (who conducted the obedience to authority experiments) and others, known collectively as the "small world experiment," laid the foundations for this (Milgram, 1967). Milgram himself never used the phrase "six degrees of separation."
26 Much of the research focuses on the internet. This has grown so enormously that Barabási (2002, p. 150) speaks of discoverers instead of designers.
27 The following two paragraphs owe a great deal to Gleick (1987; English translation 1991).
28 Lorenz originally used the example of a seagull.
29 This idea was developed and demonstrated by the Belgian physical chemist Ilya Prigogine, who received the Nobel Prize for it in 1977.
30 This is known as "the edge of chaos," a technical term first used by computer scientist Christopher Langton; it has become a metaphor for all complex systems.
31 The concept of a tipping point was popularized by Malcolm Gladwell's book by that name (2000), but it has also been used by Crane, Granovetter, and Schelling (Sassen, 2006, p. 10).
32 Despite the question of how international actions can actually be (see Dijksterhuis, 2007). The discussion of free will takes on a totally different complexion when approached from its opposite, coercion.
33 This paragraph is primarily based on Veldman (1995, Chapter 4).
34 This is what Alderman Asscher of Amsterdam called "Frankenstein's monster" in 2008 – a conglomerate of organizations, all of which had intervened with the same youths and their families, without cooperating with one another (Van den Berg et al., 2008).

Chapter 7

1 In general there is a distinction between power and authority. Power is related to the possibility of using force; authority is based on recognition. In terms of verticality, this distinction is not important.

2 For a detailed discussion, see Van Koppen (2003), and also Derksen (2009) and other popular publications.

3 Since 1999, the national Dutch Public Prosecution Service has used the BOS/Polaris system to ensure national uniformity. This is a point system based on the seriousness of the offense. Less than 20 points results in a fine; for more than 120 points a prison term is recommended. In between are all kinds of variations, such as community service, with or without a court summons (see Taraf & Dekkers, 2005).

4 This is a much-researched question, in which some do and others do not find a "punitivity gap" (see De Keijser et al., 2007). The discussion is too extensive for my purposes here, but see my 2008b. Dekker and Van der Meer (2007) point out that trust in criminal justice varies a great deal between incidents. One failed judgement has a much greater impact than 10,000 well-handled cases.

5 This well-known characterization in Dutch history comes from the legal scholar Paul Scholten (1880-1954). He compared the Dutch Civil Code of 1838 to a large old house with many defects, but a home in which one was still comfortable – a peaceful possession.

6 Such as those asked in the standard survey question: "Do you think that in general most people are trustworthy, or that you can't be careful enough in dealing with others?" The possible answers were, "Can be trusted," "You can't be careful enough," and "Don't know" (see Schyns & Dekker, 2008).

7 Moreover Cook et al. (2005) claim, based on game theory, that a society without trust is possible.

8 Much has been written about the relation between trust and social capital; I agree with the idea that trust, like condition, can be a product of social capital (Sztompka, 1999).

9 For a cognitive analysis of this connection, see Castelfranchi and Falcone (2000): "a good theory of trust cannot be completed without a theory of control" (p. 799).

10 This is a more formal triad than that of Max Weber (1947). Weber distinguishes three forms of authority: traditional (in other words, based on strong ties), legal (spelled out and expanded with both informal and formal regulations), and charisma (what remains in a media democracy, but is increasingly difficult to achieve).

11 This was demonstrated in the famous Stanford prisoner's experiment by Haney et al. (1973). A group of students were randomly assigned to be either prison guards or prisoners, and were asked to simulate a prison situation. Within a week the experiment had to be stopped because the exercise of power had gotten out of hand (filmed as *Das Experiment*).

12 In the 1970s, Dutch sociologist De Swaan (1970) introduced the term "negotiating parenting" to describe this kind of informalization (see also Wouters, 2007).
13 *Void* should not be interpreted as *emptiness*, but rather as the absence of rules (p. 34, note 5).
14 One can argue about this claim of success. The effectiveness of policy is measured by the decrease in the safety index for the community as a whole and in various neighborhoods. Success was not generally the same (Mein et al., 2009), and statistics showed that percentages for objective and subjective security in all of the Netherlands decreased in those years (Leertouwer & Kalidien, 2009).

Chapter 8

1 Small (1998) speaks of "musicking," in which the participants (as musician or as listener) search for and find their social identity.
2 Cf. Pieters (2010, p. 42), who regards feedback as the "backbone concept of complexity."
3 This section was written in collaboration with the musician Ed Wertwijn. Its sole purpose is to give some insight into the word "improvisation."
4 For three fully elaborated cases, see Boutellier & De Groot (2010), and also Van Marissing et al. (2010).
5 For an example of network analysis, see Broekhuizen (2010).
6 This is why in a number of places I used the metaphor of the soccer field. Justice is the goalkeeper as *ultimum remedium*, organizations in risk management are the backs (e.g., police, private security), social organizations in a normative role are the midfielders (schools, housing associations, social work and the like), and the social bonds between citizens are the forwards (e.g., Boutellier, 2005; Boutellier & Van Steden, 2010).
7 Compare Luhmann's self-referential mechanism (Chapter 6).
8 Other perspectives are possible, for example, if one regards student development as central. The point is the principle of institutional ordering around core functions.
9 After the credit, economic, and national crises, this problem can now be seen in a different light.
10 Cf. the concept of "directing," which has become popular in recent years. It has also taken root in the world of Dutch governance in relation to the central role of the administration, even as local authorities gain greater latitude. Broekhuizen (2010) conducted a network analysis in an Amsterdam district that carefully mapped out the formal and informal powers in play.
11 Anorexia websites, where girls with this illness meet and encourage one another to lose even more weight, are an example of a destructive way of connecting.

12 Foucault restated this insight in his concept of *governmentality* (1991, posthumous edition), in which he includes the role of the state as an object of analysis.
13 The ultimate litmus test for a "directly-deliberative polyarchy" of collective decision-making, in which the weaker in society are also involved, is according to Burris et al. the allocation of budgets to local boards.

Concluding remarks: The dynamics of organized freedom

1 A concept from Stanley Milgram, which points out the networked character of society. See also Chapter 6, note 25.
2 Thatcher was prime minister from 1979 to 1990, and Blair from 1997 to 2007.
3 My thanks to Rally Rijksschroeff for reminding me of this concept.

Epilogue

1 For a good introduction, see DeLanda (2006).

REFERENCES

Achterhuis, H. (1998). *De erfenis van de utopie.* Baarn: Ambo

Achterhuis, H. (2008). *Met alle geweld: Een filosofische zoektocht.* Rotterdam: Lemniscaat

Ashworth, A. & L. Zedner (2008). Defending the criminal law: Reflections on the changing character of crime, procedure, and sanctions. *Journal of Criminal Law and Philosophy, 2* (1), 21-51

Asselt, M. van (2009). *Dromen van maakbaarheid: Tijd om wakker te worden.* Verwey-Jonker/SER-lezing. Den Haag: SER/Verwey-Jonker Instituut

Bakhtin, M. (1984). *Rabalais and his world.* Bloomington: Indiana University Press

Bang, H. & E. Sørensen (1999). The everyday maker: A new challenge to democratic governance. *Administrative Theory & Praxis, 21* (3), 325-341

Barabási, A. (2002). *Linked: How everything is connected to everything else and what it means for business, science and everyday life.* London: Plume/Penguin

Barkhuysen, T., W. den Ouden & J. Polak (2005). *Recht realiseren: Bijdragen rond het thema adequate naleving van rechtsregels.* Deventer: Kluwer

Bartels, L. (2006). What's the matter with 'What's the matter with Kansas'? *Quarterly Journal of Political Science, 1* (2), 201-226

Baudet, T. & M. Visser (red.). (2010). *Conservatieve vooruitgang.* Amsterdam: Bert Bakker

Bauman, Z. (1993). *Postmodern ethics.* Oxford/Cambridge: Blackwell

Bauman, Z. (1997). *Postmodernity and its discontents.* Cambridge: Polity Press

Bauman, Z. (2000). *Liquid modernity.* Cambridge: Polity Press

Bauman, Z. (2003). *Liquid love: On the fragility of human bonds.* Cambridge: Polity Press

Bauman, Z. (2005). *Liquid life.* Cambridge: Polity Press

Beck, U. (1986). *Risikogesellschaft: Auf dem Weg in eine andere Moderne.* Frankfurt am Main: Suhrkamp. Eng. vert. *Risk society: Towards a new modernity* (1992). London: Sage

Beck, U. (2002). The cosmopolitan society and its enemies. *Theory Culture Society, 19* (1-2), 17-44

Beck, U., A. Giddens & S. Lash (1994). *Reflexive modernization: Politics, tradition and aesthetics in the modern social order.* Cambridge: Polity

Becker, H. & H.E. Barnes (1961). *Social thought from Lore to science.* New York: Dover Publications

Becker, J. & P. Dekker (2005). Beeld van beleid en politiek. In Sociaal en Cultureel Planbureau, *De sociale staat van Nederland* (pp. 328-362). Den Haag: Sociaal en Cultureel Planbureau

Berg, D. van den, S. van der Goot & M.-B. Jansen (2008). *Blokkades in de jeugdzorg.* Amsterdam: z.u.

Berlin, I. (1969). Two concepts of liberty. In I. Berlin (ed.), *Four essays on liberty.* London: Oxford University Press

Bernstein, P. (1998). *Against the gods: The remarkable story of risk.* New York: Wiley

Bervoets, E., N. Koeman, V. Dijk, E. van der Torre & R. de Groot (2008). *'Wat kan hier?' Veiligheidsanalyse Rembrandtplein en Leidseplein: (Uitgaans)geweld, maatregelen, effecten.* COT, Instituut voor Veiligheids- en Crisismanagement. Den Haag: Boom Juridische uitgevers

Beus, J. de (2003). *Na de Beeldenstorm: Een beschouwing over de werking van de toeschouwersdemocratie in Nederland.* Deventer, Etty Hillesumlezing, 29 november

Bijlsma-Frankema, K. & A. Costa (2005). Understanding the trust-control nexus. *International Sociology, 20* (3), 259-282

Blokland, T. & M. Savage (2008). Social capital and networked urbanism. In T. Blokland & M. Savage (eds.), *Networked urbanism: Social capital in the city.* Hampshire: Aldershot

Blond, Ph. (2010). *Red Tory: How left and right have broken Britain and how we can fix it.* London: Faber and Faber

Boers, J., R. van Steden & H. Boutellier (2008). Het effect van positieve en negatieve factoren op veiligheidsbeleving:

Een kwantitatieve studie onder inwoners van Amsterdam. *Tijdschrift voor Veiligheid, 7* (3), 34-52

Boomkens, R. (2006). *De nieuwe wanorde: Globalisering en het einde van de maakbare samenleving.* Amsterdam: Van Gennep

Boon, A. (2009). *Straf/regels: Praktijkverhalen uit de school.* Amsterdam: Augustus

Bourdieu, P. (1986). The forms of capital. In J. Richardson (ed.), *Handbook of theory and research in the sociology of education* (pp. 241-258). New York: Greenwald Press

Boutellier, H. (1993). *Solidariteit en slachtofferschap: De morele betekenis van criminaliteit in een postmoderne cultuur* (diss.). Nijmegen: SUN, heruitgave: Amsterdam University Press, 2008

Boutellier, H. (2000). *Crime and Morality: The Significance of Criminal Justice in Post-modern Culture.* Dordrecht: Kluwer Academic Publishers.

Boutellier, H. (2002). *De veiligheidsutopie: Hedendaags onbehagen en verlangen rond misdaad en straf.* Den Haag: Boom Juridische uitgevers

Boutellier, H. (2004). *The Safety Utopia: Contemporary Discontent and Desire as to Crime and Punishment.* Dordrecht: Kluwer Academic Publishers.

Boutellier, H. (2005). *Meer dan veilig: Over bestuur, bescherming en burgerschap* (oratie). Den Haag: Boom Juridische uitgevers

Boutellier, H. (2006). Een nieuwe ordening: Een verkenning van de relatie tussen veiligheid, recht en vertrouwen. In *Recht der werkelijkheid, (26) 3,* 29-45.

Boutellier, H. (2007a). Het onbekende slachtoffer: Bespreking van: J.J.M. van Dijk, The mark of Abel: Reflections on the social labeling of victims of crime (oratie), 2006. *Tijdschrift voor Criminologie, 49* (2), 194-199

Boutellier, H. (2007b). *Nodale orde: Veiligheid en burgerschap in een netwerksamenleving* (oratie). Amsterdam: Vrije Universiteit

Boutellier, H. (2008a). De grondwet, dat ben jij! In *De grondwet herzien: 25 jaar later* (pp. 51-69). Den Haag. Ministerie van BZK

Boutellier, H. (2008b). Participatie als panacee. In *De burger als opspoorder.* OM Congres 2008 (pp. 7-33). z.u.

Boutellier, H. (2010). Lokale wanordening: Over de rol van de politie bij de inrichting van de morele ruimte. In B. van Stokkom, J. Terpstra & L. Gunther Moor (red.), *De politie en haar opdracht: De kerntakendiscussie voorbij* (pp. 191-205). Apeldoorn: Maklu

Boutellier, H. & N. Boonstra (2009). *Van presentie tot correctie: Een nieuw perspectief op samenlevingsopbouw* (Wmo Kenniscahier 4). Utrecht: Verwey-Jonker Instituut

Boutellier, H. & I. de Groot (2010). *Tussen complexiteit en slagvaardigheid: Dynamische processen in veiligheidsnetwerken.* Amsterdam: Vrije Universiteit (FSW: Dynamics of Governance)

Boutellier, H. & K. Lünnemann (2007). Burgers over rechters: Over de beleving van de rechtspraak. *Rechtstreeks, 1*, 45-62

Boutellier, H. & R. van Steden (2010). Governing nodal governance: The 'anchoring' of local security networks. In A. Crawford (ed.), *International and comparative criminal justice and urban governance.* Cambridge: Cambridge University Press

Boutellier, H. & M. Vinke (2002). *Stelselmatige intimidatie: Aangiftegedrag in politiedistrict 6.* Amsterdam: Vrije Universiteit (Afdeling Strafrecht en Criminologie)

Boutellier, H., N. Boonstra & M. Ham (red.) (2009a). *Omstreden ruimte: Over de organisatie van veiligheid en spontaniteit.* Amsterdam: Van Gennep

Boutellier, H., P. Ippel & S. Nieborg (red.). (2005). *'Veiligheid gegarandeerd' en 'privacy gered': Twee voorstelbare toekomstbeelden in Nederland anno 2030.* Utrecht: Verwey-Jonker Instituut

Boutellier, H., R. Scholte & M. Heijnen (2008). *Criminogeniteitsbeeld Amsterdam 2008.* Amsterdam: Vrije Universiteit Amsterdam (FSW: Dynamics of Governance)

Bovens, M. & A. Wille (2010). *Diplomademocratie: Over de spanning tussen meritocratie en democratie.* Amsterdam: Uitgeverij Bert Bakker

Braithwaite, V. (2004). Preface. In V. Braithwaite (ed.), *Hope, power and governance. The annals of the American Academy of Political and Social Sciences, special issue 592*, 6-15

Brink, G. van den (2002). *Mondiger of moeilijker? Een studie naar de politieke habitus van hedendaagse burgers* (WRR voorstudies en achtergronden). Den Haag: Sdu Uitgevers

Brink, G. van den (2004a). *Schets van een beschavingsoffensief. Over normen, normaliteit en normalisatie in Nederland* (WRR verkenning: 3). Amsterdam: AUP

Brink, G. van den (2004b). Hoger, harder, sneller... en de prijs die men daarvoor betaalt. In P. de Beer & C. Schuyt (red.), *Bijdragen aan waarden en normen* (WRR verkenning: 2). Amsterdam: AUP

Brink, G. van den (2006). *Van waarheid naar veiligheid: Twee lessen voor een door angst bevangen burgerij.* Amsterdam: SUN

Brink, G. van den (2007). *Moderniteit als opgave: Een antwoord aan relativisme en conservatisme.* Amsterdam: SUN

Broekhuizen, J. (2010). *Veiligheidsnetwerk drugs- en drankoverlast in Oost-Watergraafsmeer: Een sociale netwerkstudie naar de gemeentelijke regie in het veiligheidsbeleid.* Amsterdam: Vrije Universiteit (FSW: Dynamics of Governance)

Brouwer, J. & A. Schilder (2008). Wijken voor orde: Over nieuwe geboden en verboden. *RegelMaat, 3*, 88-101

Brown, T. (2004). Subcultures, pop music and politics: Skinheads and the 'Nazi rock' in England and Germany. *Journal of Social History, 38* (1), 157-178

Burris, S., M. Kempa & C. Shearing (2008). Changes in governance: A cross-disciplinary review of current scholarship. *Akron Law Review, 41* (1), 1-66

Buruma, I. (2006). *Murder in Amsterdam: The death of Theo van Gogh and the limits of tolerance.* Ned. vert. *Dood van een gezonde roker.* Amsterdam: Atlas

Cachet, A. & A. Ringeling (2005). Integraal veiligheidsbeleid: Goede bedoelingen en wat ervan terechtkwam. In E. Muller (red.), *Veiligheid: Studies over inhoud, organisatie en maatregelen* (pp. 635-663). Alphen aan den Rijn: Kluwer

Caem, B. van (2008). *Verborgen kracht: Burgerparticipatie en veiligheid in Amsterdam.* Amsterdam: Vrije Universiteit (FSW: Dynamics of Governance)

Caem, B. van, R. van Steden & H. Boutellier (2010). The 'hidden strength' of active citizenship: The involvement of local residents in public safety projects. *Submitted*

Carr, P. (2005). *Clean streets: Controlling crime, maintaining order, and building community activism*. New York: New York University Press

Castelfranchi, C. & R. Falcone (2000). Trust and control: A dialectic link. *Applied Artificial Intelligence, 14* (8), 799-823

Castells, M. (2000a). *The information age: Economy, society and culture, Vol. I: The rise of the network society* (1st edition 1996). Oxford: Blackwell

Castells, M. (2000b). *The information age: Economy, society and culture, Vol. III: End of millennium* (1st edition 1998). Oxford: Blackwell

Castells, M. (2004). *The information age: Economy, society and culture, Volume II: The power of identity* (1st edition 1997). Oxford: Blackwell

Cleiren, C. (2008). Limits to criminal law. In M. Cupido (ed.), *Limits of criminal law* (pp. 7-12). Nijmegen: Wolf Legal Publishers

Cobussen, M. (2009). Improvisation: Between the musical and the social. *Dutch Journal of Musical Theory, 14* (1), 48-55

Cook, K., R. Hardin & M. Levi (2005). *Cooperation without trust?* London: Sage

Craven, P. & B. Wellman (1973). The network city. *Sociological Inquiry, 43*, 57-88

Crawford, A. (2003). 'Contractual governance' of deviant behavior. *Journal of Law and Society, 30* (4), 479-505

Crawford, A. (2006). Networked governance and the post-regulatory state? Steering, rowing and anchoring the provision of policing and security. *Theoretical Criminology, 10* (4), 449-497

Crawford, A. (2009a). Governing through anti-social behaviour: Regulatory challenges to criminal justice. *British Journal of Criminology, 49* (6), 810-831

Crawford, A. (2009b). Criminalizing sociability through anti-social behaviour legislation: Dispersal powers, young people and the police. *Youth Justice, 9* (1), 5-26

Cuperus, R. (2009). *De wereldburger bestaat niet: Waarom de opstand der elites de samenleving ondermijnt*. Amsterdam: Bert Bakker

Daems, T. (2008). *Making sense of penal change*. Oxford: Oxford University Press (Clarendon Studies in Criminology)

Dalrymple, T. (2001). *Life at the bottom. The worldview that made the underclass*. Chicago: Ivan R. Dee.

Dalrymple, Th. (2001). *Life at the bottom: The worldview that makes the underclass*. Ned. vert. *Leven aan de onderkant. Het systeem dat de onderklasse instandhoudt* (2004). Utrecht: Spectrum

Dalrymple, Th. (2005). *Our culture, what's left of it: The mandarins and the masses*. Ned. vert. *Beschaving, of wat ervan over is*. Amsterdam: Nieuw Amsterdam

Dekker, P. & J. de Hart (2005). Goede burgers. In P. Dekker & J. de Hart (red.), *De goede burger: Tien beschouwingen over een morele categorie* (pp. 11-19). Den Haag: SCP

Dekker, P. & T. van der Meer (2007). *Vertrouwen in de rechtspraak nader onderzocht*. Den Haag: SCP

Dekker, P. & E. Steenvoorden (2008). *Continue onderzoek burgerperspectieven*. Den Haag: SCP

DeLanda, M. (2006). *A new philosophy of society: Assemblage theory and social complexity*. London: Continuum

Delden, P. van (2009). *Sterke netwerken: Ketensamenwerking in de publieke dienstverlening*. Amsterdam: Van Gennep. Gebaseerd op *Samenwerking in de publieke dienstverlening* (diss., 2009). Delft: Eburon

Derksen, A. & L. Verplanke (1987). *Geschiedenis van de onmaatschappelijkheidsbestrijding in Nederland 1914-1970*. Amsterdam/Meppel: Boom

Derksen, O. (2009). *Het O.M. in de fout*. Diemen: Veen Magazines

Dijk, J. van (1999). The one-dimensional network society of Manuel Castells. *New Media and Society, 1* (1), 127-138

Dijk, J. van (2005). *The deepening divide: Inequality in the information society*. London: Sage

Dijk, J. van (2006). *The network society* (2nd edition; oorspronkelijke titel *De netwerkmaatschappij*, 1991). London: Sage
Dijk, J.J.M. van (2008a). *Slachtoffers als zondebokken*. Apeldoorn: Maklu
Dijk, J.J.M. van (2008b). *The world of crime: Breaking the silence on problems of security, justice and development across the world*. London: Sage
Dijk, J.J.M. van & J. de Waard (2009). Forty years of crime prevention in the Dutch Polder. In A. Crawford (ed.), *Crime prevention policies in comparative perspective* (pp. 130-152). Cullompton: Willan Publishing
Dijksterhuis, A. (2007). *Het slimme onbewuste: Denken met gevoel*. Amsterdam: Bert Bakker
Dohmen, J. (2007). *Tegen de onverschilligheid: Pleidooi voor een moderne levenskunst*. Amsterdam: Ambo
Dohmen, J. (2008). *Het leven als kunstwerk: Een hartstochtelijk pleidooi voor een stijlvol en waarachtig leven*. Diemen: Lemniscaat
Durkheim, E. (1893). *De la division du travail social*. Eng. vert. *The rules of sociological method and selected texts on sociology and its methods* (1982). London: MacMillan
Durkheim, E. (1906). *Détermination du fait moral*. Ned. vert. De bepaling van het morele feit. In E. Durkheim, *Over moraliteit* (1977). Amsterdam/Meppel: Boom
Duyvendak, J., E. Engelen & I. de Haan (2008). *Het bange Nederland: Pleidooi voor een open samenleving*. Amsterdam: Bert Bakker
Elffers, H. & W. de Jong (2004). 'Nee, ik voel me nooit onveilig': Determinanten van sociale onveiligheidsgevoelens. In Raad voor Maatschappelijke Ontwikkeling, *Sociale veiligheid organiseren: Naar herkenbaarheid in de publieke ruimte* (Advies 31, Bijlage 5). Den Haag: Sdu Uitgevers
Ellickson, R. (1991). *Order without law. How neighbors settle disputes* (2nd edition 1994). London: Harvard University Press

Enzensberger, H. (1992). *Die Große Wanderung. 33 Markierungen. Mit einer Fußnote 'Über einige Besonderheiten bei der Menschenjagd'.* Frankfurt am Main: Suhrkamp

Ericson, R. (2007). *Crime in an insecure world.* Cambridge: Polity Press

Eshun, K. (1998). *More brilliant than the sun: Adventures in sonic fiction.* London: Quartet Books

Etzioni, A. (1996). *The new golden rule: Community and morality in a democratic society.* Ned. vert. *De nieuwe gulden regel: Gemeenschap en moraal in een democratische samenleving* (2005). Kampen: Ten Have

Faulks, K. (2000). *Citizenship.* London: Routledge

Feeley, M. & J. Simon (1994). Actuarial justice: The emerging new criminal law. In D. Nelken (ed.), *The futures of criminology.* London: Sage

Felson, M. (1998). *Crime and everyday life.* Thousand Oaks: Pine Forge Press

Ferrell, J. & C. Sanders (1995). *Cultural criminology.* Boston: Northeastern University Press

Field, F. (2003). *Neighbours from hell: The politics of behaviour.* London: Politico's

Fiers, L. & A. Jansen (2004). *Het succes van buurtbemiddeling: Resultaten van het evaluatieonderzoek.* Utrecht: Expertisecentrum Buurtbemiddeling

Foerster, H. von & G. Pask (1961). A predictive model for self-organizing systems. Part I: *Cybernetica, 3,* 258-300; Part II: *Cybernetica, 4,* 20-55

Fortuyn, P. (2002). *Verweesde samenleving: Een religieus-sociologisch traktaat.* Uithoorn: Karakter Uitgevers

Foucault, M. (1977). *Discipline and punishment: The birth of the prison.* London: Allen Lane

Foucault, M. (1991). Governmentality. In G. Burchell, C. Gordon & P. Miller (eds.), *The Foucault effect: Studies in governmentality* (pp. 87-104). Hemel Hempstead: Harvester Wheatsheaf

Frank, Th. (2004). *What's the matter with Kansas: How conservatives won the heart of America.* New York: Metropolitan Books

Frank, Th. (2008). *The wrecking crew: How conservatives ruined government, enriched themselves and beggared the nation.* New York: Metropolitan Books

Franke, H. (1990). *Twee eeuwen gevangen: Misdaad en straf in Nederland.* Utrecht: Spectrum

Franke, H. (2005). *The emancipation of prisoners. A socio-historical analysis of the Dutch prison experience.* Edinburgh: Edinburgh University Press.

Friedman, T. (2005). *The world is flat: A brief history of the twenty-first century.* Ned. vert. *De aarde is plat: Ontdekkingsreis door een geglobaliseerde wereld.* Amsterdam: Nieuw Amsterdam

Frissen, P. (2007). *De staat van verschil: Een kritiek van gelijkheid.* Amsterdam: Van Gennep

Fromm, E. (1941). *Escape from freedom.* Ned. vert. *Angst voor de vrijheid* (1952). Utrecht: Erven J. Bijleveld

Fukuyama, F. (1992). *The end of history and the last man.* Ned. vert. *Het einde van de geschiedenis en de laatste mens.* Amsterdam: Contact

Fukuyama, F. (1995). *Trust: The social virtues and the creation of prosperity.* New York: Free Press

Fung, A. & E. Wright (2001). Deepening democracy: Innovations in empowered participatory governance. *Politics & Society, 29* (1), 5-41

Furedi, Fr. (1997). *Culture of fear, risk-taking and the morality of low expectation.* London: Continuum, heruitgave 2002

Garland, D. (1996). The limits of sovereign state: Strategies of crime control in contemporary societies. *British Journal of Criminology, 36* (4), 445-471

Garland, D. (2001). *The culture of control: Crime and social order in contemporary society.* Oxford: Oxford University Press

Giddens, A. (1991). *Modernity and self-identity: Self and society in the late modern age.* Cambridge: Polity

Gielen, A.-J. (2008). *Radicalisering en identiteit: Radicale rechtse en moslimjongeren vergeleken.* Amsterdam: Aksant

Gladwell, M. (2000). *The tipping point: How little things can make a big difference.* London: Little Brown

Gleick, J. (1987). *Caos: La nascita di una nuova scienza*. Eng. vert. *Chaos: Making a new science* (1991). New York: Viking Penguin

Goffman, E. (1974). *Frame analysis: An essay on the organization of experience*. New York: Harper & Row

Gramsci, A. (1971). *Selections from the Prison Notebooks*. New York: International Publishers.

Gramsci, A. (1972). *Marxisme als filosofie van de praxis* (een bloemlezing, samengesteld, ingeleid en vertaald door Yvonne Scholten). Amsterdam: Van Gennep

Granovetter, M. (1973). The strength of weak ties. *The American Journal of Sociology, 78* (6), 1360-1380

Granovetter, M. (1978). Threshold models of collective behavior. *American Journal of Sociology, 83* (6), 1420-1443

Gray, J. (2007). *Black mass: Apocalyptic religion and the death of Utopia*. London: Allen Lane. Ned. vert. *Zwarte mis: Religieus fundamentalisme en de moderne utopieën*. Amsterdam: Ambo

Gruijter, M. de, E. Smits van Waesberghe & H. Boutellier (2010). *Een vreemde in eigen land: Boze autochtone burgers over nieuwe Nederlanders en de overheid*. Amsterdam: Aksant

Gunsteren, H.R. van (1988). Admission to citizenship. *Ethics*, 98 (4): 731-741

Gunsteren, H. van (1998). *Theory of citizenship: Organizing plurality in contemporary democracies*. Boulder: Westview Press

Gunsteren, H. van (2006). *Vertrouwen in democratie: Over de principes van zelforganisatie*. Amsterdam: Van Gennep

Haan, W. de (2003). In een kwaad daglicht – de toestand in de Nederlandse criminologie besproken door dr. J.C.J. Boutellier. *Tijdschrift voor Criminologie, 45* (1), 71-79

Hageman, H. (2008). *Tussen controle en vertrouwen: Een casestudy naar de aanpak van overlast in de Transvaalbuurt*. Amsterdam: Vrije Universiteit (FSW: Dynamics of Governance)

Hajer, M. (2009). *Authoritative governance: Policy making in the age of mediatization*. Oxford: Oxford University Press

Hall, St., S. Winlow & Cr. Ancrum (2008). *Criminal identities and consumer culture: Crime, exclusion and the new culture of narcissism*. Cullompton: Willan

Hammer, F. (2009). *Wild west web? Over digitale eigenrichting en handvatten voor slachtoffers* (scriptie). Universiteit Utrecht: Rechtenfaculteit

Haney, C., W. Banks & P. Zimbardo (1973). Interpersonal dynamics in a simulated prison. *International Journal of Criminology and Penology, 1*, 69-97

Heath, J. & A. Potter (2004). *The rebel sell: How the counterculture became consumer culture.* London: Capstone

Hill, C. & E. Lynn (2005). Is hierarchical governance in decline? Evidence from empirical research. *Journal of Public Administration Research and Theory, 15* (2), 173-195

Hiltz, S. & M. Turoff (1978). *The network nation: Human communication via computer.* Reading: Addison-Wesley

Hirsch Ballin, E. (1994). *In ernst: Oriëntaties voor beleid.* Den Haag: Sdu Uitgevers

Hobbs, D., P. Hadfield, S. Winlow, S. Lister & S. Hall (2000). Receiving shadows: Governance and liminality in the night time economy. *British Journal of Sociology, 51* (4), 701-717

Hof, Chr. van 't, R. van Est & Fl. Daemen (2010). *Check in / Check uit: De digitalisering van de openbare ruimte.* Den Haag: Rathenau Instituut

Huberts, L. (2005). *Integriteit en integritisme in bestuur en samenleving: Wie de schoen past…* (oratie). Amsterdam: Vrije Universiteit (FSW)

Huberts, L., F. Anechiarico & F. Six (eds.). (2008). *Local integrity systems.* Den Haag: Boom Juridische uitgevers

Innes, M. (2004). Reinventing tradition? Reassurance, neighbourhood security and policing. *Criminal Justice, 4* (2), 151-171

Jong, J. de (2007). *Kapot moeilijk: Een etnografisch onderzoek naar opvallend delinquent groepsgedrag van 'Marokkaanse' jongens.* Amsterdam: Aksant

Katz, J. & R. Rice (2002). *Social consequences of internet use: Access, involvement, and interaction.* Cambridge: The MIT Press

Keijser, J. de, P. van Koppen & H. Elffers (2007). Bridging the gap between judges and the public? A multi-method study. *Journal of Experimental Criminology, 3*, 131-161

Kempen, P. van (2008). Veiligheid is geen mensenrecht. In *NRC Handelsblad*, Opinie & debat (20/21 december, p. 2)

Kennedy, J. (1995). *Nieuw Babylon in aanbouw: Nederland in de jaren zestig*. Amsterdam: Boom

Kernfield, B. (1995). *What to listen for in jazz*. New Haven: Yale University Press

Kinneging, A. (1997). *Aristocracy, antiquity and history: An essay on classicism in political thought* (diss.). New Brunswick: New Brunswick Translation Publishers

Kinneging, A. (2000). Het conservatisme, kritiek van de Verlichting en de moderniteit. *Philosophia Reformata, 2*, 126-153

Kinneging, A. (2005). *Geografie van goed en kwaad: Filosofische essays*. Utrecht: Spectrum

Klijn, E. & J. Koppenjan (1994). Beleidsnetwerken als theoretische benadering: Een tussenbalans. *Beleidswetenschap, 11* (2), 143-167

Komter, A. (2003). *Solidariteit en de gift*. Eng. vert. *Solidarity and the gift* (2005). Cambridge: Cambridge University Press.

Koops, B.-J., C. Lüthy, A. Nelis & C. Sieburgh (red.). (2009). *De maakbare mens: Tussen fictie en fascinatie*. Amsterdam: Bert Bakker

Koppen, P. van (2003). *De Schiedammer parkmoord: Een rechtspsychologische reconstructie*. Nijmegen: Ars Aequi Libri.

Kroes, P. (2006). *Projecten waarbij politie en burgers samenwerken op het gebied van de veiligheidszorg* (ongepubliceerd). Apeldoorn: Mediatheek Politieacademie

Krol, G. (1990). *Voor wie kwaad wil. Een bespiegeling over de doodstraf*. Amsterdam: Querido

Krol, G. (1998). De ondraaglijke lichtheid van sommige straffen. In *Grenzen tussen goed en kwaad: 13 essays over preventie, misdaad en straf in de 21e eeuw*. Den Haag: Ministerie van Justitie

Krol, G. (2000). *De vitalist*. Amsterdam: Querido

Kruglanski, A., X. Chen, M. Dechesne, S. Fishman & E. Orehek (2009). Fully committed: Suicide bombers' motivation and the quest for personal significance. *Political Psychology, 30*, 331-357

Lans, J. van der (2005). *Koning burger: Nederland als zelfbedieningszaak*. Amsterdam: Augustus

Leertouwer, E. & S. Kalidien (2009). De strafrechtsketen in samenhang. In S. Kalidien & A. Eggen (red.), *Criminaliteit en rechtshandhaving 2008: Ontwikkelingen en samenhangen* (pp. 201-239). Den Haag: CBS/WODC/Boom

Lindblom, Ch. (1959). The science of muddling through. *Public Administration Review, 19*, 79-88

Lint, W. de & S. Kirta (2004). Security in ambiguity: Towards a radical security politics. *Theoretical Criminology, 8* (4), 465-489

Loader, I. (2008). The anti-politics of crime. *Theoretical Criminology, 12* (3), 399-410

Loader, I. & N. Walker (2006). Necessary virtues: The legitimate place of the state in the production of security. In B. Dupont & J. Woods (eds.), *Democracy, society and the governance of security* (pp. 165-196). Cambridge: Cambridge University Press

Lorenz, E. (1979). *Predictability: Does the flap of a butterfly's wings in Brazil set off a tornado in Texas?* Address at the annual meeting of the American Association for the Advancement of Science in Washington, December 29, 1979

Low, S. (2003). *Behind the gates: Life, security and the pursuit of happiness in fortress America*. London: Routledge

Luhmann, N. (1990). *Essays on self-reference*. New York: Columbia University Press

Luiten, M. (2006). Moeizaam moraliseren op het VMBO. In E. Tonkens, J. Uitermark & M. Ham (red.), *Handboek moraliseren: Burgerschap en ongedeelde moraal* (hoofdstuk 3). Amsterdam: Van Gennep

Lünnemann, K. (2007). *Risicoscreening in de vrouwenopvang*. Utrecht: Verwey-Jonker Instituut

Lünnemann, K., F. de Meere & S. ter Woerds (2008a). *Het raadplegen van burgers: Op zoek naar een kader voor*

burgerraadpleging door het Openbaar Ministerie. Utrecht: Verwey-Jonker Instituut
Lünnemann, K., M. Moll & S. ter Woerds (2008b). *Burgers geraadpleegd: Burgers over straftoemetingsrichtlijnen*. Utrecht: Verwey-Jonker Instituut
Lyon, D. (2001). *Surveillance society: Monitoring everyday life*. Buckingham: Open University Press
Lyon, D. (2007). *Surveillance studies: An overview*. Cambridge: Polity Press
MacIntyre, A. (1981). *After virtue: A study in moral theory* (2nd edition 1984). Notre Dame: University of Notre Dame Press
Mak, J., A. Huygen, M. Steketee & H. Jonkman (2010). *Opgroeien in veilige wijken: Evaluatie van communities that care in Maassluis, Hoogvliet en Leiden-Stevenshof*. Utrecht: Verwey-Jonker Instituut
Marissing, E. van, S. Tan & H. Boutellier (2010). *'Het is hier net Amsterdam': Een veiligheidsarrangement voor IJburg*. Utrecht: Verwey-Jonker Instituut
Martin, J. (1978). *The wired society: A challenge for tomorrow*. Englewood Cliffs, NJ: Prentice Hall
Maruna, Sh., A. Matravers & A. King (2004). Disowning our shadow: A psychoanalytic approach to understanding punitive public attitudes. *Deviant Behavior, 25*, 277-299
Maturana, H. & F. Varela (1980). *Autopoiesis and cognition*. Dordrecht: Reidel
Mein, A., F. de Meere & R. van Wonderen (2009). *Analyse Rotterdamse veiligheidsindex: Eindrapportage*. Utrecht: Verwey-Jonker Instituut
Meurs, P. (2008). *Sociaal vertrouwen: Een kwestie van durf?* Den Haag/Utrecht: SER/Verwey-Jonker Instituut
Milgram, S. (1967). The small world problem. *Psychology Today, 2*, 60-67
Mill, J. (1859). On liberty. In E. Robson (ed.), *Collected works* (Vol XVIII, 1977). Toronto: University of Toronto Press
Ministerie van AZ (2004). *Kabinetsreactie op het WRR-rapport 'Waarden, normen en last van het gedrag'*. Kamerstukken II 2003/2004, 29 452, nr. 2

Ministerie van BZK en Ministerie van Justitie (2002). *Naar een veiliger samenleving.* Den Haag: Ministerie van BZK

Ministerie van Justitie (1985). *Samenleving en criminaliteit: Een beleidsplan voor de komende jaren.* Den Haag: Ministerie van Justitie

Ministerie van Justitie (2009a). *Justitie = sociale cohesie.* Den Haag: Ministerie van Justitie

Ministerie van Justitie (2009b). *Samen effectief: De praktijk als inspiratie* (brochure). Den Haag: Ministerie van Justitie

Minister van WWI (2009). *Integratiebrief aan de Tweede Kamer.* Den Haag: Ministerie van WWI, Directie I&I

Mol, A. (2006). *De logica van het zorgen: Actieve patiënten en de grenzen van het kiezen.* Amsterdam: Van Gennep

Mooij, A. (1975). *Taal en verlangen: Lacans theorie van de psychoanalyse.* Meppel: Boom

Nederland, T., A. Huygen & H. Boutellier (2009). *Governance in de Wmo: Theorie en praktijk van vernieuwende governance modellen* (Wmo Kenniscahier 3). Utrecht: Verwey-Jonker Instituut

Nexus (2004). Europa realiseren. Tien conclusies voor de politieke leiders van de Europese Unie. *Nexus, 40,* 11-17

Noije, L. van & K. Wittebrood (2008). *Sociale veiligheid ontsleuteld: Veronderstelde en werkelijke effecten van Veiligheidsbeleid.* Den Haag: SCP

Noordegraaf, M. (2004). *Management in het publieke domein: Issues, instituties en instrumenten.* Bussum: Coutinho

O'Malley, P. (2004). *Risk, uncertainty and government.* London: The Glasshouse Press

Ombudsman van Rotterdam (2007). *Baas in eigen huis: Rapport van een ambtshalve onderzoek naar de praktijk van huisbezoeken.* Rotterdam: Publicatie Ombudsman van Rotterdam

Ossewaarde, R. (2007). Waarom hedendaagse elites geen burgerschap kunnen overdragen. In K. van Beek & M. Ham (red.), *Gaat de elite ons redden? De nieuwe rol van de bovenlaag in onze samenleving* (pp. 139-153). Amsterdam: Van Gennep

Overbeek, R. van, C. Scholten, D. Oudenampsen, M. Moll & V. Leckie (2008). *Inzet van menselijk kapitaal: Vrijwilligers en hun werk bij patiënten- en gehandicaptenorganisaties.* Utrecht: Verwey-Jonker Instituut/Vilans

Overeem, P. (2010). Alasdair MacIntyre. In Th. Baudet & M. Visser (red.), *Conservatieve vooruitgang* (hoofdstuk 20). Amsterdam: Prometheus

Pels, D. (2005). *Een zwak voor Nederland: Ideeën voor een nieuwe politiek.* Amsterdam: Anthos

Peper, B. (1998). *Sociale problemen en de moderne samenleving: Een cultuursociologische beschouwing.* Amsterdam: Het Spinhuis

Pieterman, R. (2008). *De voorzorgcultuur: Streven naar veiligheid in een wereld vol risico en onzekerheid.* Den Haag: Boom Juridische uitgevers

Pieters, K. (2010). *Into complexity: A pattern-oriented approach to stakeholder communications* (diss.). Utrecht: Universiteit voor Humanistiek

Power, M. (1994). *The audit explosion.* London: Demos

Power, M. (2004), *The risk management of everything.* London: Demos

Power, M. (2007). *Organized uncertainty: Designing a world of risk management.* Oxford: Oxford University Press

Presdee, M. (2000). *Cultural criminology and the carnival of crime.* London: Routledge

Projectgroep Visie op de politiefunctie (2005). *Politie in ontwikkeling: Visie op de politiefunctie.* Den Haag: NPI

Putnam, R. (2000). *Bowling alone: The collapse and revival of American community.* New York: Touchstone

Putnam, R., R. Leonardi & R. Nanetti (1992). *Making democracy work: Civic traditions in modern Italy.* Princeton: Princeton University Press

Reich, R. (2007). *Supercapitalism: The transformation of business, democracy, and everyday life.* Ned vert. *Superkapitalisme en de bedreiging voor onze democratie.* Amsterdam: Business Contact

Reiner, R. (2006). Beyond risk: A lament for social democratic criminology. In T. Newborn & P. Rock (eds.), *The politics of crime control* (pp. 7-51). Oxford: Oxford University Press
Rhodes, R. (1994). The hollowing out of the state: The changing nature of the public service in Britain. *Political Quarterly, 65* (2), 138-151
Robertson, R. (1992). *Globalization: Social theory and global culture*. London: Sage
Roels, S. (2005). *Security: An inquiry into the character of a value that dominates today's society*. Utrecht: Universiteit Utrecht, Department of Philosophy
Romein, E., M. Schuilenburg & S. van Tuinen (2009). *Deleuze compendium*. Amsterdam: Boom
Rorty, R. (1986). Freud and moral reflection. In J. Smith & W. Kerrigan (eds.), *Pragmatism's Freud: The moral disposition of psychoanalysis* (pp. 1-20). Baltimore: John Hopkins University Press
Rorty, R. (1989). *Contingency, irony, and solidarity*. Cambridge: Cambridge University Press
Rosanvallon, P. & A. Goldhammer (2008). *Counter democracy: Politics in an age of distrust*. Cambridge: Cambridge University Press
Rosenthal, U. (1988). *Aan de orde van de dag: Opstellen over orde en veiligheid*. Alphen aan den Rijn: Samson
Rothstein, B. (2000). Trust, social dilemmas and collective memories. *Journal of Theoretical Politics, 12* (4), 477-501
Rothstein, B. (2005). *Social traps and the problem of trust*. Cambridge: Cambridge University Press
Ruller, S. van (1993). Het irrationele van strafrechtelijke sancties. *Tijdschrift voor Criminologie, 4*, 336-350
Sassen, S. (2006). *Territory, authority, rights from medieval to global assemblages*. New York: Princeton University Press
Scheffer, P. (2007). *Het land van aankomst*. Amsterdam: De Bezige Bij
Schinkel, W. (2008). *Denken in een tijd van sociale hypochondrie: Aanzet tot een theorie voorbij de maatschappij*. Kampen: Klement

Scholte, R. (2008). Burgerparticipatie in veiligheidsprojecten: Een empirische verkenning. In H. Boutellier & R. van Steden (red.), *Veiligheid en burgerschap in een netwerksamenleving* (pp. 223-241). Den Haag: Boom Juridische uitgevers

Schuilenburg, M. & P. van Calster (2009). De collectieve winkelontzegging: Een antwoord van willekeur op overlast. In H. Boutellier, N. Boonstra & M. Ham (red.), *Omstreden ruimte: Over de organisatie van veiligheid en spontaniteit* (pp. 137-155). Amsterdam: Van Gennep

Schuyt, K. (2006). *Steunberen van de samenleving: Sociologische essays*. Amsterdam: AUP

Schyns, P. & P. Dekker (2008). Sociale cohesie in de publieke opinie. In P. Schnabel, R. Bijl & J. de Hart (red.), *Betrekkelijke betrokkenheid: Studies in sociale cohesie* (pp. 33-60). Den Haag: SCP

Scruton, R. (2007). *Culture counts: Faith and feeling in a world besieged*. New York: Encounter Books

Sennett, R. (1998). *The corrosion of character*. Ned. vert. *De flexibele mens: Psychogram van de moderne samenleving* (2000). Den Haag: Bzztôh

Shearing, C. & J. Wood (2003). Nodal governance: Democracy and the new 'denizens'. *Journal of law & Society, 30* (3), 400-419

Siegel, D., F. van Gemert & F. Bovenkerk (red.). (2009). *Culturele criminologie*. Den Haag: Boom Juridische uitgevers

Simon, J. (2007). *Governing through crime: How the war on crime transformed American democracy and created a culture of fear*. Oxford: Oxford University Press

Sloterdijk, P. (2006). *Zorn und Zeit: Politisch-psychologischer Versuch*. Ned vert. *Woede en tijd: Een politiek-psychologisch essay* (2007). Amsterdam: SUN

Sloterdijk, P. (2010) *Rage and time. A psychopolitical investigation*. New York: Columbia University Press. English translation of *Zorn und Zeit Politisch-psychologischer Versuch* (2006).

Small, C. (1998). *Musicking: The meanings of performing and listening*. Hanover: Wesleyan/University Press of New England

Smith, M. (2007). *The right talk: How conservatives transformed the great society into the economic society*. Princeton: Princeton University Press

Spangenberg, F., M. Lampert, M. Moerland, H. Boerboom & L. Knoop (2001). *Burgerschapsstijlen en overheidscommunicatie* (niet gepubliceerd). Amsterdam: Motivaction

Spithoven, R. (2010). *Niet bang maar onzeker: Vijf benaderingen van sociale onveiligheid in een risicoaverse samenleving* (scriptie). Amsterdam: Vrije Universiteit

Spruyt, B. (2003). *Lof van het conservatisme*. Amsterdam: Balans

Steden, R. van (2009). De pretparksamenleving: Een wereld van veilig vertier. In H. Boutellier, N. Boonstra & M. Ham (red.), *Omstreden ruimte: Over de organisatie van spontaniteit en veiligheid* (pp. 15-32). Amsterdam: Van Gennep

Steden, R. van (2010). Sturing van sociale veiligheid. In R. van Steden (red.), *Sturing van lokale veiligheid: Een achtergrondstudie en drie reflecties*. Amsterdam/Den Haag: VU/NICIS

Steden, R. van & T. Jones (2008). Straatcoaches in Slotervaart: Enige kanttekeningen bij het idee van een 'overheid op afstand'. *Tijdschrift voor Veiligheid, 7* (4): 20-29

Stewart, A. (1995). Two conceptions of citizenship. *The British Journal of Sociology, 46* (1), 63-78

Stewart, P. (2001). Complexity theories, social theory, and the question of social complexity. *Philosophy of the Social Sciences, 31*, 323-360

Stokkom, B. van (2008). Bange burgers, doortastende dienstverleners: Voorbij de retoriek van burgerschap en zelfredzaamheid. In H. Boutellier & R. van Steden (red.), *Veiligheid en burgerschap in een netwerksamenleving* (pp. 267-289). Den Haag: Boom Juridische uitgevers

Stokkom, B. van (2010). *Wat een hufter! Ergernis, lichtgeraaktheid en maatschappelijke verruwing*. Amsterdam: Boom

Stone, Cl. (1989). *Regime politics: Governing Atlanta 1946-1988*. Kansas: Lawrence University Press

Strogatz, St. (2003). *Sync: The emerging science of spontaneous order* (edition 2004). London: Penguin Books

Swaan, A. de (1979). Uitgaansbeperking en uitgaansangst: Over de verschuiving van bevelshuishouding naar onderhandelingshuishouding (oratie). In *De mens is de mens een zorg: Opstellen 1971-1981* (1982, pp. 81-115). Amsterdam: Meulenhof
Swaaningen, R. van (1996). Justitie als verzekeringsmaatschappij: 'Actuarial justice' in Nederland. *Justitiële verkenningen, 5*, 80-97
Sztompka, P. (1999). *Trust: A sociological theory*. Cambridge: Cambridge University Press
Sztompka, P. (2002). On the decaying moral space: Is there a way out? *European Review, 10* (1), 63-72
Tanenhaus, S. (2009). *The death of conservatism*. New York: Random House
Taraf, S. & M. Dekkers (2005). *Evaluatie BOS/Polaris* (stagerapport). Amsterdam: UvA
Taylor, C. (2004). *Modern social imaginaries*. Durham: Duke University Press
Taylor, C. (2007). *A secular age*. Cambridge: The Belknap Press of Harvard University Press
Taylor, F. (1911). *Principles of scientific management*. New York: Harper & brothers
Terpstra, J. (2008). Burgers in veiligheid: Lokale netwerken en buurtcoalities. In H. Boutellier & R. van Steden (red.), *Veiligheid en burgerschap in een netwerksamenleving* (pp. 243-265). Den Haag: Boom Juridische uitgevers
Terpstra, J. & R. Kouwenhoven (2004). *Samenwerking en netwerken in de lokale veiligheidszorg*. Enschede: UT/P&W/IPIT
Tinkebell, K. & C. Vogelaar (z.j. circa 2009). *Dearest Tinkebell*. Amsterdam: TORCH Gallery
Tonkens, E. (2008). *Mondige burgers, getemde professionals*. Amsterdam: Van Gennep
Tonkens, E., M. Hurenkamp & J. Duyvendak (2006a). *Wat burgers bezielt: Een onderzoek naar burgerinitiatieven*. Amsterdam: UvA/NICIS

Tonkens, E., M. Uitermark & M. Ham (red.). (2006b). *Handboek moraliseren: Burgerschap en ongedeelde moraal* (Jaarboek TSS). Amsterdam: Van Gennep

Tönnies, F. (1887). *Gemeinschaft und Gesellschaft*. Ned. vert. *Gemeenschap en maatschappij* (1990). Leuven: Acco

Tops, P. (2007). *Regimeverandering in Rotterdam: Hoe een stadsbestuur zichzelf opnieuw uitvond*. Amsterdam: Atlas

Turkle, Sh. (1984). *The second self: Computers and the human spirit*. London: Granada

Urry, J. (2003). *Global complexity*. Cambridge: Polity Press

Veldman, A. (1995). *Effectuering van sociaal-economisch recht volgens de chaostheorie: Beleidsinstrumentering en rechtshandhaving van (supra)nationaal gelijkebehandelingsrecht* (diss.). Utrecht: Universiteit Utrecht

Verhoeven, I. (2004). Veranderend politiek burgerschap en democratie. In E. Engelen & M. Sie Dhian Ho (red.), *De staat van de democratie: Democratie voorbij de staat* (pp. 119-143). Amsterdam: AUP

Verhoeven, I. (2009). *Burgers tegen beleid: Een analyse van dynamiek in politieke betrokkenheid*. Amsterdam: Aksant

Verwey-Jonker Instituut (2010). Bedreigers van politici: Risico's en interventiemogelijkheden. In *Individuele bedreigers van publieke personen in Nederland: Fenomeenanalyse en een beleidsverkenning* (pp. 24-91). Den Haag: NCTb

Vollaard, B., P. Versteegh & J. van den Brakel (2009). *Veelbelovende verklaringen voor de daling van de criminaliteit na 2002*, in opdracht van Politie & Wetenschap (vooralsnog niet gepubliceerd), te vinden op www.uvt.nl/webwijs/show/?uid=b.a.vollaard

Vuyk, K. (2006). *Het menselijk teveel: Over de kunst van het leven en de waarde van de kunst*. Kampen: Klement

Vuysje, H. (1989). *Lof der dwang*. Amsterdam: Anthos/Bosch & Keuning

Wacquant, L. (2009). *Punishing the poor: The neoliberal government of social insecurity*. Durham: Duke University Press

Wæver, O. (1995). Securitization and desecuritization. In R. Lipschutz (ed.), *On security* (pp. 46-86). New York: Columbia University Press
Walker, R. (1989). *The coherence theory of truth: Realism, anti-realism, idealism*. London: Routledge
Walzer, M. (2004). *Politics and passion: Toward a more egalitarian liberalism*. New Haven: Yale University Press
Watts, D. (2003). *Six degrees: The science of a connected age*. New York: Norton
Weber, M. (1947). *The theory of social and economic organization*. New York: The Free Press
Wetenschappelijke Raad voor het Regeringsbeleid (2003). *Waarden, normen en de last van gedrag*. Amsterdam: AUP
Wetenschappelijke Raad voor het Regeringsbeleid (2007). *Identificatie met Nederland* (Rapporten aan de regering 79). Amsterdam: AUP
Wetenschappelijke Raad voor het Regeringsbeleid (2008). *Onzekere veiligheid* (Rapporten aan de regering 82). Amsterdam: AUP
Wetenschappelijke Raad voor het Regeringsbeleid (2009). *Vertrouwen in de school: Over de uitval van 'overbelaste' jongeren* (WRR 83). Amsterdam: AUP
Winter, M. de (2005). *Democratieopvoeding versus de code van de straat* (oratie). Utrecht: Universiteit van Utrecht
Witteveen, W. (2008). Nomoi: Plato en de regelzucht. *RegelMaat, 3*, 105-110
Wolf, N. (2007). *The shock doctrine: The rise of disaster capitalism*. New York: Metropolitan Books
Wouters, C. (2007). *Informalization: Manners and emotions since 1890*. London: Sage. Ned. vert. *Informalisering: Manieren en emoties sinds 1890* (2008). Amsterdam: Bert Bakker
Wrong, D. (1995). *The problem of order: What unites and divides society*. Boston: Harvard University Press
Young, M. (1958). *The rise of the meritocracy, 1870-2033: An essay on education and inequality*. London: Thames & Hudson
Zedner, L. (2007). Pre-crime and post-criminology? *Theoretical Criminology, 11* (2), 261-281

Zedner, L. (2009). *Security*. London: Routledge

Zuijlen, R. van (2004). Veiligheid als begrip: Fundering van de rechtsorde. In E. Muller (red.), *Veiligheid: Studies over inhoud, organisatie en maatregelen* (pp. 7-24). Alphen aan den Rijn: Kluwer

Zuurmond, A. (1994). *De infocratie: Een theoretische en empirische heroriëntatie op Weber's ideaaltype in het informatietijdperk.* Den Haag: Phaedrus